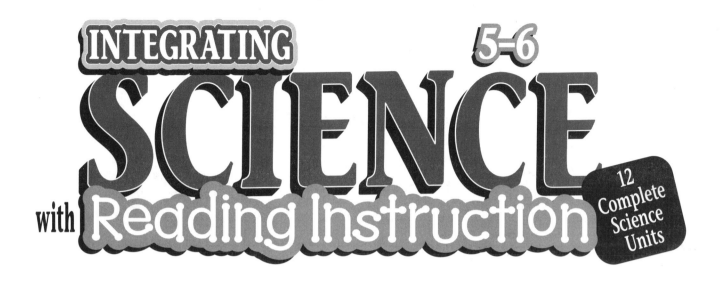

INTEGRATING SCIENCE 5-6 with Reading Instruction

12 Complete Science Units

Written by
Trisha Callella and Marilyn Marks

PARENT-TEACHER COLLECTION

Editor: LaDawn Walter
Illustrator: Jenny Campbell
Cover Illustrator: Rick Grayson
Designer/Production: Moonhee Pak/Terri Lamadrid
Cover Designer: Moonhee Pak
Art Director: Tom Cochrane
Project Director: Carolea Williams

Reprinted 2007
© 2002 Creative Teaching Press, Inc., Huntington Beach, CA 92649

Table of Contents

Introduction

For many students, reading comprehension diminishes when they read nonfiction text. Students often have difficulty understanding scientific vocabulary, making inferences, and grasping scientific concepts. With so much curriculum to cover each day, science is sometimes put on the back burner when it comes to academic priorities. *Integrating Science with Reading Instruction 5–6* provides the perfect integration of science content with specific reading instruction to help students improve their comprehension of nonfiction text and maximize every minute of your teaching day.

This resource includes twelve units that cover three areas of science—life, earth, and physical. The units are based on the most common science topics taught in grades 5–6 in accordance with the National Science Education Standards:

Life Science	**Earth Science**	**Physical Science**
Ecosystems	Phases of the Moon	Pulleys
Animal Classification	Outer Space	Heat Energy
Photosynthesis	Weathering and Erosion	Physical and Chemical Changes
Body Systems	Energy from the Earth	Elements and Compounds

Each unit includes powerful prereading strategies, such as predicting what the story will be about, accessing prior knowledge, and brainstorming about vocabulary that may be included in the reading selection. Following the prereading exercises is a nonfiction reading selection written on a grade 5–6 reading level. Each reading selection is followed by essential postreading activities such as comprehension questions on multiple taxonomy levels, skill reviews, and a critical thinking exercise. Each unit also includes a hands-on science experiment that follows the scientific method. The descriptions on pages 5–8 include the objectives and implementation strategies for each unit component.

Before, during, and after reading the story, students are exposed to the same reading strategies you typically reinforce during your language arts instruction block. This powerful duo gives you the opportunity to teach both reading and science simultaneously. Using the activities in this resource, students will continue *learning to read* while *reading to learn*. They will become more successful readers while gaining new science knowledge and experiences.

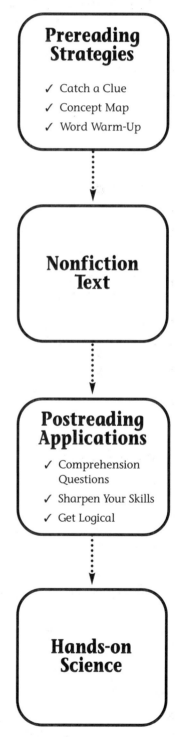

Prereading Strategies
- ✓ Catch a Clue
- ✓ Concept Map
- ✓ Word Warm-Up

Nonfiction Text

Postreading Applications
- ✓ Comprehension Questions
- ✓ Sharpen Your Skills
- ✓ Get Logical

Hands-on Science

Connections to Standards

This chart shows the National Science Education Standards that are covered in each unit.

LIFE SCIENCE	Eco-systems	Animal Classification	Photo-synthesis	Body Systems
Living systems at all levels of organization demonstrate the balance of structure and function.	●	●	●	●
Plants and animals have structures for respiration, digestion, waste disposal, and transport of materials.			●	●
Cells carry on the many functions needed to sustain life.			●	●
Each type of cell, tissue, and organ has a distinct structure and set of functions that serve the organism as a whole.			●	●
The human organism has systems that interact with one another.				●
The major source of energy is sunlight for ecosystems.	●		●	
Millions of species of animals, plants, and microorganisms are alive today.	●	●		

EARTH SCIENCE	Phases of the Moon	Outer Space	Weathering and Erosion	Energy from the Earth
Land forms are the result of a combination of constructive and destructive forces.			●	
The topography of the earth's surface is reshaped by the weathering and erosion of rock and soil.			●	
The earth is connected to the solar system in many ways.		●		
Most objects in the solar system are in regular and predictable motion.	●	●		
Natural energy and material resources are classified into renewable and nonrenewable resources.				●
The sun is a major source of energy for occurrences on the earth's surface.				●

PHYSICAL SCIENCE	Pulleys	Heat Energy	Physical and Chemical Changes	Elements and Compounds
A substance has characteristic properties.			●	●
A mixture of substances can often be separated into the original substances.			●	●
Substances react chemically with other substances to form new compounds.			●	●
Energy is a property of many substances.	●	●	●	●
Energy is transferred in many ways.	●	●	●	●
Heat moves in predictable ways.		●		

Unit Overview

Catch a Clue

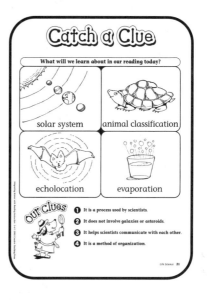

Objectives

Students will

✓ be introduced to key concepts and vocabulary *before* reading

✓ be able to transfer this key strategy to improve test-taking skills

Implementation

Students will use clues and the process of elimination to predict what the nonfiction reading selection will be about. Copy this page on an overhead transparency, and use it for a whole-class activity. Begin by reading aloud each word, and ask students to repeat the words. Read the clues one at a time. Then, discuss with the class what topic(s) could be eliminated and the reasons why. (Note: There will be clues that do not eliminate any topics. The purpose of this is to teach students that although there is information listed, it is not always helpful information.) Cross off a topic when the class decides that it does not fit the clues. If there is more than one topic left after the class discusses all of the clues, this becomes a prediction activity. When this occurs, reread the clues with the class, and discuss which answer would be most appropriate given the clues provided.

Concept Map

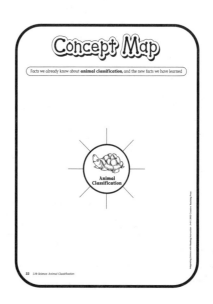

Objectives

Students will

✓ access prior knowledge by brainstorming what they already know about the topic

✓ increase familiarity with the science content by hearing others' prior knowledge experiences

✓ revisit the map *after* reading to recall information from the reading selection

Implementation

Copy this page on an overhead transparency, and use it for a whole-class activity. Use a colored pen to write students' prior knowledge on the transparency. After the class reads the story, use a different colored pen to add what students learned.

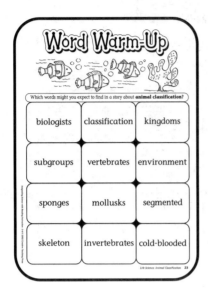

Word Warm-Up

Objectives

Students will

✓ be introduced to new vocabulary words

✓ make predictions about the story using thinking and reasoning skills

✓ begin to monitor their own comprehension

Implementation

Students will use the strategy of exclusion brainstorming to identify which words are likely to be in the story and which words are unrelated and should be eliminated from the list. Copy this page on an overhead transparency, and use it for a whole-class activity. Have students make predictions about which of the vocabulary words could be in the story and which words probably would not be in the story. Ask them to give reasons for their predictions. For example, say *Do you think sponges would be part of animal classification?* A student may say *Yes, because they are invertebrates* or *No, because they are used to clean the kitchen sink.* Circle the word if a student says that it will be in the story, and cross it out if a student says it will not be in the story. Do not correct students' responses. After reading, students can either confirm or disconfirm their own predictions. It is more powerful for students to verify their predictions on their own than to be told the answer before ever reading the story.

Nonfiction Text

The Story

Objectives

Students will

✓ read high-interest, nonfiction stories

✓ increase science knowledge

✓ increase content area vocabulary

✓ make connections between the science facts and their own experiences

Implementation

Give each student a copy of the story, and display the corresponding Word Warm-Up transparency while you read the story with the class. After the class reads the story, go back to the transparency, and have students discuss their predictions in relation to the new information they learned in the story. Invite students to identify any changes they would make on the transparency and give reasons for their responses. Then, revisit the corresponding Concept Map transparency, and write the new information students have learned.

Postreading Applications

Comprehension Questions

Objectives

Students will

✓ recall factual information

✓ be challenged to think beyond the story facts to make inferences

✓ connect the story to other reading, their own lives, and the world around them

Implementation

Use these questions to facilitate a class discussion of the story. Choose the number and types of questions that best meet the abilities of your class.

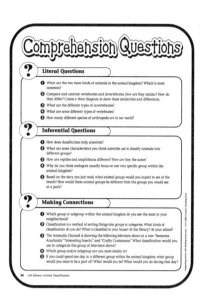

Sharpen Your Skills

Objectives

Students will

✓ practice answering questions in common test-taking formats

✓ integrate language arts skills with science knowledge

Implementation

After the class reads a story, give each student a copy of this page. Ask students to read each question and all of the answer choices for that question before deciding on an answer. Show them how to use their pencil to completely fill in the circle for their answer. Invite students to raise their hand if they have difficulty reading a question and/or the answer choices. Thoroughly explain the types of questions and exactly what is being asked the first few times students use this reproducible.

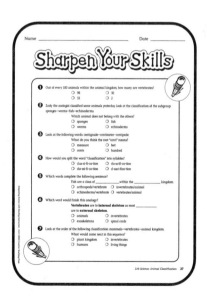

Get Logical

Objectives

Students will

✓ practice logical and strategic thinking skills

✓ practice the skill of process of elimination

✓ transfer the information read by applying it to new situations

Implementation

Give each student a copy of this page. Read the beginning sentences and the clues to familiarize students with the words. Show students step-by-step how to eliminate choices based on the clues given. Have students place an X in a box that represents an impossible choice, thereby narrowing down the options for accurate choices. Once students understand the concept, they can work independently on this reproducible.

Hands-on Science

Science Experiment

Objectives

Students will

✓ participate in hands-on learning experiences

✓ apply the scientific method

✓ expand and reinforce science knowledge

✓ apply new science vocabulary words

Implementation

Each experiment begins with a scientific question. Encourage students to brainstorm answers (hypotheses) and discuss their ideas based on facts they learned from the reading selection. (Additional teacher background information and experiment results are provided to enhance discussions.) Help students focus on the idea that most relates to the upcoming experiment. Review the step-by-step procedure for the hands-on experiment with the class, and provide them with the necessary materials for the activity. Give each student a copy of the corresponding reproducible that uses the steps of the scientific method. Have students read and follow the directions as they conduct the experiment. Discuss the questions in the Results and Conclusions section, and have students write their answers on their page. The final question in this section restates the inquiry used to start the activity.

Catch a Clue

What will we learn about in our reading today?

habitats

ecosystems

endangered species

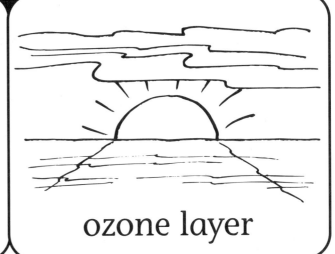

ozone layer

Our Clues

1 It is related to the category of life science.

2 It involves living things.

3 We will learn about locations and characteristics of the climate.

4 It involves different places in the world where living things coexist.

5 It includes plants, animals, and their environments.

Concept Map

Facts we already know about **ecosystems,** and the new facts we have learned

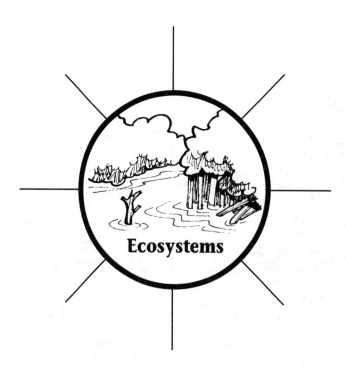

Ecosystems

Integrating Science with Reading Instruction · 5–6 © 2002 Creative Teaching Press

Word Warm-Up

Which words might you expect to find in a story about **ecosystems?**

irrigation	habitat	polluting
interact	hardwood	weather
marshes	minerals	global
transporting	forest	recreation

Ecosystems

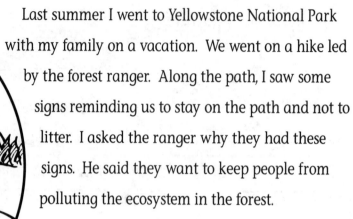

Last summer I went to Yellowstone National Park with my family on a vacation. We went on a hike led by the forest ranger. Along the path, I saw some signs reminding us to stay on the path and not to litter. I asked the ranger why they had these signs. He said they want to keep people from polluting the ecosystem in the forest.

"What is an ecosystem?" I asked.

The ranger went on to explain that ecosystems are groups of life forms that interact with each other and the nonliving parts of the environment. He said there are several different ecosystems. Each ecosystem has a particular type of climate and even different types of soil. Some are found where it is hot and dry, others where it is cool and moist, and others can be cold and dry. The types of ecosystems are forest, coastal, desert, grassland, tundra, freshwater, and ocean.

My curiosity was stirred, so I asked, "If there are different ecosystems, does that mean they also have different types of plants and animals that live in each one?"

"Yes, there are!" the ranger answered with excitement. Before I could say anything else, he began to talk more about the ecosystems. He explained that there are three different types of forest ecosystems. They are hardwood, evergreen, and tropical rain forest. Hardwood and evergreen forests are cool and moist. This allows a lot of trees to grow there. Wood, honey, mushrooms, fruit, nuts, and drinking and irrigation water are some of the things the hardwood and evergreen forests give us. He told me the weather was the opposite in the tropical rain forest. It is hot and very wet there. I was shocked when he told me it rains over 100 inches (2.54 m) there every year! He explained that tropical rain forests help clean the air, provide homes for wildlife, and supply us with fruits, nuts, and medicines.

Integrating Science with Reading Instruction · 5–6 © 2002 Creative Teaching Press

"Boy, this ranger knows a lot!" I thought to myself. So I asked him to describe more to me about the other types of ecosystems. He started with the coastal ecosystems.

"They are mostly marshes and swamps," he said. "They give us fish, shellfish, salt, seaweed, and other resources. They provide a habitat for wildlife and harbors for transporting goods, and they dilute and treat waste." He went on to explain that the oceans cover almost three-fourths of the Earth. There are many different ecosystems in the ocean. Some are in shallow water, and others are in deeper water. The oceans serve as a means of transportation and places for recreation and supply us with lots of fish and shellfish to eat.

He told me how deserts are very dry and hot. "Even though it only rains less than 10 inches (25 cm) a year, the deserts provide homes for some wildlife," he said in a happy voice. "They also provide us with useful things like salt, oil, and minerals."

I continued to learn many new facts as he talked about the grassland ecosystems. The weather is mild and pretty dry there. He said the reason they are called grasslands is because they do not get enough water for many trees to grow and are covered with grasses instead. We receive much of our food from managed grassland ecosystems like the farm. The grasslands also give us animal products like wool and leather.

"You might like to visit the wilderness grasslands in the savanna of Africa someday," he said. "You can see many types of interesting wildlife there! We are almost at the end of our hike so I will quickly finish explaining the rest of the ecosystems." He explained that tundra ecosystems have freezing cold and dry weather. They provide homes for wildlife and many other living things. They also give us oil and minerals. The freshwater ecosystems include ponds, lakes, and rivers. They give us fish and drinking water. They also are a way of transportation and help dilute and carry away waste.

"I sure learned a lot from you," I said to the ranger. "Thank you for teaching me so much! I will be sure to pass the message on to my friends to help keep people from polluting."

Integrating Science with Reading Instruction · 5–6 © 2002 Creative Teaching Press

Comprehension Questions

? Literal Questions

1. What is an ecosystem?
2. How are ecosystems different based on their location?
3. What are the three different types of forest ecosystems?
4. How are the tropical rain forests beneficial?
5. Which ecosystems provide a home for wildlife?

? Inferential Questions

1. Which type of land ecosystem do you think would have the fewest types of wildlife living there? The most? Why?
2. Deserts are the driest ecosystems. Using what you learned from the story, which other ecosystem do you think is often found near deserts? Why?
3. The ocean has several ecosystems—some in shallow water, and others in deeper water. Why can't the same plants and animals live in shallow and deep water? How do you think these environments would be different?
4. Why do you think evergreen forests and hardwood forests are named the way they are?
5. If tropical rain forests are always hot and very wet, in what regions on a globe do you think you would find them?

? Making Connections

1. What ecosystems have you visited before? How would you describe the climate of the ecosystems you visited?
2. Why do you need to know what ecosystems are, where they are located, and how to preserve them?
3. If you go to a coastal ecosystem, what would you expect to see?
4. What type of ecosystem is the closest to where you live?
5. Why has Smokey the Bear been so popular for so many years? What is he trying to promote? Why?

Integrating Science with Reading Instruction · 5–6 © 2002 Creative Teaching Press

Sharpen Your Skills

1 Researchers have been **tracking** the climate for many years.
   Which word is a synonym for the word "tracking"?
   ○ following   ○ researching
   ○ wasting   ○ collecting

2 If you wanted to learn more about the different locations of the world's ecosystems and the animals that live in each place, which resource would be the most helpful?
   ○ almanac   ○ atlas
   ○ dictionary   ○ encyclopedia

3 The **alarming** results show that precipitation is decreasing and overall temperatures throughout the year are increasing.
   In this sentence, what part of speech is the word "alarming"?
   ○ adjective   ○ adverb
   ○ preposition   ○ conjunction

4 Which words would finish this analogy?
   Coastal ecosystem is to _____ as **forest ecosystem** is to _____.
   ○ honey/shellfish   ○ seaweed/oil
   ○ wood/nitrogen   ○ salt/honey

5 Don't look so **bored!** Go get your lap **board,** and draw a picture of your favorite ecosystem.
   What type of words are "bored" and "board"?
   ○ synonyms   ○ homonyms
   ○ antonyms   ○ heteronyms

6 If you saw the guide words "echo–envious," which word would <u>not</u> be found on those pages of the dictionary?
   ○ environment   ○ ecology
   ○ engineer   ○ efficient

7 Which punctuation mark is used to show dialogue in the story?
   ○ exclamation point ○ period
   ○ quotation marks   ○ colon

Integrating Science with Reading Instruction · 5–6 © 2002 Creative Teaching Press

Name _____   Date _____

 Get Logical

Mrs. Johnson's class was preparing group reports on different ecosystems. Steven, Michelle, Sheri, Joe, and Lenny were chosen as group leaders. Each group will be researching one of the following five topics: desert, tundra, coastal ecosystems, ocean, or tropical rain forest. Use the clues below to decide which topic each group will report on.

Clues

❶ Joe's group is learning about a dry ecosystem.

❷ Michelle's group discovered it rains some almost every day in their ecosystem.

❸ Steven's group learned their ecosystem is so cold that the ground stays frozen for most of the year.

❹ Sheri's group is learning about things that live in the water.

❺ Lenny's group discovered that whales, seals, and many types of fish inhabit their ecosystem.

	Joe	Michelle	Steven	Sheri	Lenny
Desert					
Tundra					
Coastal Ecosystems					
Ocean					
Tropical Rain Forest					

Joe's group reported on the _____.

Michelle's group reported on the _____.

Steven's group reported on the _____.

Sheri's group reported on the _____.

Lenny's group reported on the _____.

Integrating Science with Reading Instruction · 5–6 © 2002 Creative Teaching Press

Ecosystems

How would climate and the type of soil influence plants that live in an ecosystem?

Teacher Background Information

The nonliving parts of an environment, such as the amount of available sunlight and water, temperature range, and the type of soil, have a big influence on what types of plants will be able to live there. You will find different types of plants living in different ecosystems. Obviously, more organisms will be found living where the climate is more suitable to their needs.

Desert ecosystems are hot and dry, but they do experience a wide range in temperature as it gets much colder at night. Desert soil tends to be sandy and rocky. Grassland ecosystems are considered mild and fairly dry, as they receive around 15–35 inches (38–88.9 cm) of rain a year. The soil is richer due to higher humus content from decayed plants and animals. Hardwood (deciduous) and evergreen (coniferous) forests are cool and moist. Each forest receives around 35–70 inches (88.9–177.8 cm) of rain a year. More moisture falls as snow in the evergreen forest, while more falls as rain in the hardwood forest. Tropical rain forest ecosystems are among the most productive. These areas are hot and humid all year long, since these rain forests are located near the equator. Many rain forests receive 150–200 or more inches (381–508 cm) of rain a year. Tundra ecosystems are much harsher environments. Most of the ground is frozen all year, and only 3–6 inches (7.5–15 cm) thaw out during a short spring and summer.

In this experiment, you can fit several loaf pans onto each cookie sheet. (This is to collect any extra water that drains out.) Just be sure one cookie sheet is for all of the "desert" loaf pans, and the other one is for all of the "grassland" loaf pans.

Experiment Results

When students record information on their Ecosystems Growth Chart (page 19), they should try to include some descriptive terms rather than just a general term such as "grew well." They might include descriptions of the color of the cactus and note any changes in firmness, the estimated percentage of grass seeds that sprouted, or the height. They should note that the amount of water used in the desert container had an adverse effect on the grass but not the cactus. Conversely, the amount of water in the grassland container may have caused the cactus to become soft or even start to rot, while the grass seeds thrived with more moisture. The difference in the soil will cause the water to drain away more quickly (in the desert) or to be absorbed better (in the grassland). This will definitely influence the growth of both the cactus and the grass. The students should be able to conclude that grass will grow better in the grassland and the cactus will grow better in the desert.

Ecosystems

How would climate and the type of soil influence plants that live in an ecosystem?

Procedure

1 Use a nail to carefully poke ten holes in the bottom of each aluminum loaf pan.

2 Fill one pan with potting soil. Write *Grassland* and your names on a piece of masking tape. Place the tape on the pan.

3 Fill the other pan two-thirds full of sand. Fill the remainder of the pan with potting soil. Mix the sand and soil together. Write *Desert* and your names on a piece of masking tape. Place the tape on the pan.

4 Plant one small cactus in each pan.

5 Scatter 1 teaspoon of grass seed over the surface of the soil in BOTH pans.

6 Place each pan on a separate cookie sheet.

7 Pour water in each pan. (The soil should be moist but not soggy.)

8 Place the cookie sheets together in a sunny location so the loaf pans will receive the same amount of light.

9 Add water to the "grassland" pan twice a week. (Again, the soil should be moist but not soggy.)

10 Add water to the "desert" pan once every other week. Allow the soil to dry out between waterings.

11 Observe the growth of the grass and cactus plants for one month, and record your results on your Ecosystems Growth Chart.

MATERIALS

(per group)

- ✔ Ecosystems Growth Chart (page 19)
- ✔ nail
- ✔ 2 medium-sized, disposable aluminum loaf pans
- ✔ potting soil
- ✔ masking tape
- ✔ sand
- ✔ 2 small cactus plants
- ✔ teaspoon
- ✔ grass seed
- ✔ 2 cookie sheets (for the class to share)
- ✔ water

Grassland

Integrating Science with Reading Instruction · 5–6 © 2002 Creative Teaching Press

Ecosystems Growth Chart

How would climate and the type of soil influence plants that live in an ecosystem?

Directions: Record your observations in the chart below. Tell what happened to the grass and the cactus plants.

Grassland

Date	Amount Watered	Observations (growth and changes in cactus and grass)

Desert

Date	Amount Watered	Observations (growth and changes in cactus and grass)

Name _____   Date _____

Ecosystems

How would climate and the type of soil influence plants that live in an ecosystem?

Results and Conclusions

1 How did the amount of water affect the growth of the grass in the desert pan?

_____

2 How did the amount of water affect the growth of the cactus in the desert pan?

_____

3 How did the amount of water affect the growth of the grass in the grassland pan?

_____

4 How did the amount of water affect the growth of the cactus in the grassland pan?

_____

5 Do you think the difference in soil had an effect on the growth of the cactus? _____ Why or why not?

_____

6 Do you think the difference in soil had an effect on the growth of the grass? _____ Why or why not?

_____

7 In which ecosystem will grass grow better?

_____

8 In which ecosystem will the cactus grow better?

_____

9 How would climate and the type of soil influence plants that live in an ecosystem?

_____

Integrating Science with Reading Instruction · 5–6 © 2002 Creative Teaching Press

Catch a Clue

Integrating Science with Reading Instruction · 5–6 © 2002 Creative Teaching Press

What will we learn about in our reading today?

solar system

animal classification

echolocation

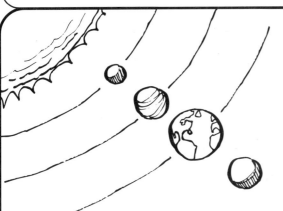

evaporation

Our Clues

1 It is a process used by scientists.

2 It does not involve galaxies or asteroids.

3 It helps scientists communicate with each other.

4 It is a method of organization.

Concept Map

Facts we already know about **animal classification,** and the new facts we have learned

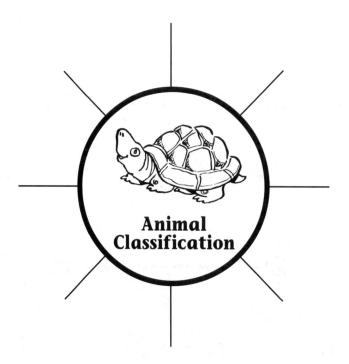

**Animal
Classification**

Integrating Science with Reading Instruction · 5–6 © 2002 Creative Teaching Press

Word Warm-Up

Which words might you expect to find in a story about **animal classification?**

biologists	classification	kingdoms
subgroups	vertebrates	environment
sponges	mollusks	segmented
skeleton	invertebrates	cold-blooded

Animal Classification

Did you know that there are possibly 10 million different types of animals living on our planet Earth? With so many different types, how do you think biologists can keep them straight? They use a process called classification. Classification is a way to put things that are alike in groups, or "kingdoms." The animal kingdom is divided into groups and then into subgroups. There are two main groups of animals: vertebrates and invertebrates. Vertebrates are animals with an internal skeleton. Invertebrates are animals without backbones.

More than 98% of all the animal species in the world are invertebrates. All invertebrates are cold-blooded. This means they cannot control their own body temperature. They depend on their environment to stay warm. The simplest invertebrate animals are the sponges. They filter water to remove tiny plants and animals. Most sponges live in salt water, but there are a few freshwater sponges. Soft, cup-shaped water creatures are another type of invertebrate. They have stinging cells on their tentacles. Some well-known cup-shaped animals are jellyfish, sea anemones, and coral.

Worms are another type of invertebrate. Worms are grouped according to their shape. There are flatworms, roundworms, and segmented worms. The common earthworm is a segmented worm. Echinoderms are another group. They are spiny-skinned animals. Echinoderms are unusual because you cannot tell their front from their back. Their body parts branch out from the center of their body like spokes on a wheel. They have a hard, shell-like, spiny covering on the outside of their body. Some echinoderms are sand dollars, sea urchins, and sea stars. All echinoderms live in the ocean. Mollusks are another group. They are seashell animals. Most mollusks have thick, soft bodies that are protected by hard shells. They are found living on land and in freshwater and salt water. Clams, snails, and squid are some types of mollusks.

Integrating Science with Reading Instruction · 5–6 © 2002 Creative Teaching Press

The largest invertebrate group contains all of the arthropods. Did you know that scientists have found about 9 million different species of arthropods in our world? Arthropods have a hard exoskeleton and jointed legs. There are five classes, or categories, of arthropods: insects, crustaceans, arachnids, centipedes, and millipedes. Most of the animals that we call "bugs" are really arthropods. One way to tell them apart is by the number of legs they have. Crustaceans, like crabs and shrimp, have ten legs. Arachnids, which include spiders, ticks, and scorpions, have eight legs. Insects have six legs. Centipedes and millipedes have lots of legs. Their bodies are made of sections. Centipedes have one pair of legs per section, and millipedes have two pairs of legs per section.

Vertebrates are the smallest group in the animal kingdom. However, it is the group we know the most about. Vertebrates have five classes: fish, amphibians, reptiles, birds, and mammals. Fish are cold-blooded vertebrates that breathe through gills. They are covered with wet, slippery scales, and most lay eggs. Amphibians have smooth skin that must stay moist. They hatch from eggs and are cold-blooded. Amphibians, such as frogs, toads, and salamanders, experience metamorphosis during their lifetime. Most adult amphibians live mainly on land. Reptiles have dry scales and dry skin, breathe with lungs, are cold-blooded, and most hatch from leathery eggs. Snakes, turtles, lizards, alligators and crocodiles are common reptiles. Birds are warm-blooded vertebrates that hatch from hard-shelled eggs, are covered with feathers, breathe with lungs, and have wings. They have a beak, no teeth, and a strong skeleton made of many hollow bones. Ducks, hawks, robins, and eagles are all birds that can fly. The ostrich and penguin are some birds that do not fly. Mammals are warm-blooded vertebrates that breathe with lungs. They have babies that are born alive and nursed by their mother's milk. Mammals are covered with skin and hair. Some mammals have a lot of hair, or fur. Other mammals, like whales, have very little hair. Scientists classify mammals as the highest form of life. Can you guess what group you are classified under?

Integrating Science with Reading Instruction · 5–6 © 2002 Creative Teaching Press

Comprehension Questions

Literal Questions

❶ What are the two main kinds of animals in the animal kingdom? Which is most common?

❷ Compare and contrast vertebrates and invertebrates. How are they similar? How do they differ? Create a Venn diagram to show these similarities and differences.

❸ What are the different types of invertebrates?

❹ What are some different types of vertebrates?

❺ How many different species of arthropods are in our world?

Inferential Questions

❶ How does classification help scientists?

❷ What are some characteristics you think scientists use to classify animals into different groups?

❸ How are reptiles and amphibians different? How are they the same?

❹ Why do you think zoologists usually focus on one very specific group within the animal kingdom?

❺ Based on the story you just read, what animal groups would you expect to see at the beach? How would these animal groups be different from the groups you would see at a park?

Making Connections

❶ Which group or subgroup within the animal kingdom do you see the most in your neighborhood?

❷ Classification is a method of sorting things into groups or categories. What kinds of classification do you do? What is classified in your house? At the library? At your school?

❸ The Animalia Channel is showing the following television shows in a row: "Awesome Arachnids," "Interesting Insects," and "Crafty Crustaceans." What classification would you use to categorize this group of television shows?

❹ Which group and/or subgroup are you most similar to?

❺ If you could spend one day in a different group within the animal kingdom, what group would you want to be a part of? What would you be? What would you do during that day?

Integrating Science with Reading Instruction · 5-6 © 2002 Creative Teaching Press

Sharpen Your Skills

1 Out of every 100 animals within the animal kingdom, how many are vertebrates?

- ○ 98
- ○ 50
- ○ 33
- ○ 2

2 Zody the zoologist classified some animals yesterday. Look at the classification of the subgroup: sponges–worms–fish–echinoderms.

Which animal does not belong with the others?

- ○ sponges
- ○ fish
- ○ worms
- ○ echinoderms

3 Look at the following words: centigrade–centimeter–centipede.

What do you think the root "centi" means?

- ○ measure
- ○ feet
- ○ cents
- ○ hundred

4 How would you split the word "classification" into syllables?

- ○ clas-si-fi-ca-tion
- ○ cla-ss-ifi-ca-tion
- ○ cla-ssi-fi-ca-tion
- ○ cl-ass-i-fica-tion

5 Which words complete the following sentence?

Fish are a class of _____ within the _____ kingdom.

- ○ arthropods/vertebrate
- ○ invertebrates/animal
- ○ echinoderms/vertebrate
- ○ vertebrates/animal

6 Which word would finish this analogy?

Vertebrates are to **internal skeleton** as most _____ are to **external skeleton.**

- ○ animals
- ○ invertebrates
- ○ exoskeletons
- ○ spinal cords

7 Look at the order of the following classification: mammals–vertebrates–animal kingdom.

What would come next in this sequence?

- ○ plant kingdom
- ○ invertebrates
- ○ humans
- ○ living things

Integrating Science with Reading Instruction · 5–6 © 2002 Creative Teaching Press

Name _____   Date _____

Get Logical

The Pet Place is almost ready for its grand opening. It plans to feature unusual pets and animals from around the world. The owners want the layout for the display cases to be organized so that the customers and visitors can locate the animals they are interested in. Each wall is a different color—red, blue, green, orange, and yellow. Five creatures still need to be displayed—millipedes, rabbits, salamanders, sponges, and ostrich. Use the clues below to decide where each animal should be displayed.

Clues

❶ A bird that cannot fly would be displayed on the orange wall.

❷ The millipedes would not be displayed on the red or the green wall.

❸ The amphibians are all displayed on the yellow wall.

❹ The mammals are not on the blue or green wall.

❺ The sponges are not on the red or blue wall.

	Millipedes	Rabbits	Salamanders	Sponges	Ostrich
Red Wall					
Blue Wall					
Green Wall					
Orange Wall					
Yellow Wall					

The millipedes should go on the _____.

The rabbits should go on the _____.

The salamanders should go on the _____.

The sponges should go on the _____.

The ostrich should go on the _____.

Integrating Science with Reading Instruction · 5–6 © 2002 Creative Teaching Press

Animal Classification

What are some features scientists use to classify animals?

Teacher Background Information

Scientists classify all living things into five kingdoms—monerans, protists, fungi, plants, and animals. In many ways, the animal kingdom seems more complex than the other kingdoms. There are more subdivisions within the animal kingdom, and more animal species have been identified. The main idea upper-grade elementary students should learn is that scientists classify living things based on their external, physical characteristics (e.g., shape, number of appendages, body covering), as well as their internal structure (e.g., skeleton, complexity of organ systems, method of reproduction). Simple invertebrates, like sponges and jellyfish, have bodies made of only two layers of cells and no developed organ systems. Worms are a little more complex. They have simple nervous and digestive systems. The annelid worms are more advanced. They have circulatory, excretory, and reproductive systems as well. As you progress up through the vertebrates, the internal structures become better developed and more complex. That is why mammals are considered the highest form of animal life.

For the experiment, it will be easier if you place the fish on the disposable pie plate and the earthworm in a small dish and cover it with plastic wrap *before* you distribute these materials to the student groups. Sea sponges are available at art and hardware stores, and you can find earthworms at most pet stores. Ask the butcher at the market to cut the fish in half lengthwise.

Experiment Results

Students should note on their Animal Classification Chart (page 31) that all of the animals except the fish are invertebrates. The sponge and earthworm have no legs. The sponge may feel soft, springy, or slightly rough (depending on the type). The earthworm should feel soft, smooth, and moist. Careful observations might reveal tiny whiskers (called setae) on the underside, which aid in crawling. They should be able to observe that spiders have two sections to their body, eight legs (which are attached to the head section), and no antennae; whereas, insects have three sections to their body, six legs (attached to the midsection or thorax), and antennae. The holes in the sponge allow water to pass through. The water is filtered to remove tiny plant and animal food. In addition to the different number of body parts, in question 2 students most likely will indicate that insects have antennae whereas spiders do not. They might also mention that insects have large compound eyes and spiders have simple eyes (usually about eight). Fish are covered with wet scales, which provide protection. The fish is classified differently from all of the other animals because it has a backbone; it is a vertebrate animal. The fish's gills are used for breathing.

Integrating Science with Reading Instruction · 5–6 © 2002 Creative Teaching Press

Animal Classification

What are some features scientists use to classify animals?

Procedure

1 Use the magnifying glass to carefully observe the external features of each animal. Notice if the animal has any appendages (i.e., arms or legs), how many sections or parts form the body, and what the animal is covered with or how it feels.

2 Feel the sea sponge. Observe the many tunnels and holes.

3 Remove the plastic wrap from the small dish. Pick up the earthworm, and examine it more closely. Then, return it to the covered dish.

4 Observe the spider. Compare and contrast it with the insect.

5 Remove the plastic wrap from the aluminum pie plate. Look outside and inside the fish. Feel the body surface. Observe the backbone and internal gill openings.

6 Wash your hands, and dry them with a paper towel.

7 Record your observations on your Animal Classification Chart.

MATERIALS

(per group)
- ✔ Animal Classification Chart (page 31)
- ✔ magnifying glass
- ✔ sea sponge
- ✔ earthworm
- ✔ plastic spider and ant (or other insect)
- ✔ fish cut in half
- ✔ disposable aluminum pie plate
- ✔ small dish
- ✔ plastic wrap
- ✔ paper towels

Integrating Science with Reading Instruction • 5–6 © 2002 Creative Teaching Press

Animal Classification Chart

What are some features scientists use to classify animals?

Animal	Vertebrate or Invertebrate?	Legs? How Many?	How Does It Feel? (e.g., soft, hard, wet, dry)
Sea Sponge			
Earthworm			
Spider			
Insect			
Fish			

Integrating Science with Reading Instruction · 5–6 © 2002 Creative Teaching Press

Name _____   Date _____

Animal Classification

What are some features scientists use to classify animals?

Results and Conclusions

❶ What do you think the tunnels and holes in a sea sponge are for?

_____

❷ How many body sections does a spider have? _____ An insect? _____

What is another way a spider and an insect are different?

_____

❸ What is covering the fish's body?

_____

What do you think these are for?

_____

❹ What is the main reason a fish is classified differently from all the other animals you observed?

_____

❺ Why does a fish have gills?

_____

❻ What are some features scientists use to classify animals?

_____

Integrating Science with Reading Instruction · 5–6 © 2002 Creative Teaching Press

Catch a Clue

What will we learn about in our reading today?

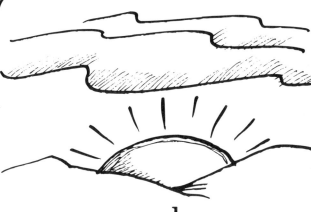

simple machines

electrical currents

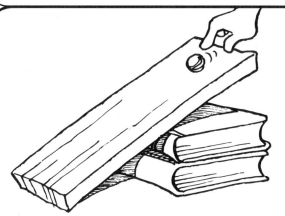

ozone layer

photosynthesis

Our Clues

1 It involves things that act like elevators.

2 It occurs naturally.

3 It requires light.

4 It affects the air we breathe.

5 Plants do this.

Integrating Science with Reading Instruction • 5–6 © 2002 Creative Teaching Press

Concept Map

Facts we already know about **photosynthesis,** and the new facts we have learned

Integrating Science with Reading Instruction · 5–6 © 2002 Creative Teaching Press

Word Warm-Up

Carbon Dioxide

Water

Sunlight

Glucose

Which words might you expect to find in a story about **photosynthesis?**

elements	absorbed	carbon dioxide
skeleton	energy	sugar
elevators	oxygen	veins
pigment	compounds	proteins

Integrating Science with Reading Instruction · 5–6 © 2002 Creative Teaching Press

Photosynthesis

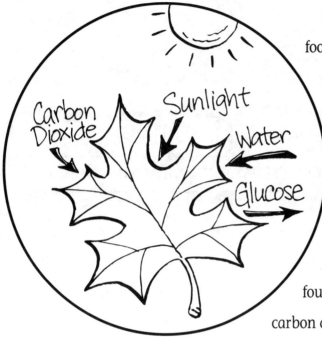

Did you know that green plants make their own food? Of all the living things in our natural world, green plants are the only things that can make their own food. This process is called photosynthesis. Synthesis means "putting together or making something." The prefix "photo" means light. Therefore, the word photosynthesis means "to make something with light."

In order for photosynthesis to happen, four elements must be present. They are chlorophyll, carbon dioxide, water, and solar energy. All plants contain chlorophyll. This is a green pigment (color) found mainly in the leaves. Chlorophyll is what gives a plant its color. Carbon dioxide is a gas in the air. It enters the leaves through very tiny openings called stomata. The stomata are mainly found on the underside of the leaves. Plants absorb water through their roots. The water is carried up to the leaves and other parts of the plant through special tubes, called xylem. The xylem tubes can be thought of as "up elevators" because they carry water and minerals up the plant. The solar energy comes from the sun.

There are many steps that take place during photosynthesis. The first is for the chlorophyll to trap the sun's energy. Then, the carbon dioxide that enters the leaves is combined with the water. This makes a simple sugar and the extra oxygen is released from the plant. The simple sugar travels to all parts of the plant through special tubes called phloem. You can think of the phloem tubes as "down elevators" because their job is to carry food that is made in the leaves down to other parts of the plant, including the stem and roots. The phloem tubes and the xylem tubes are bundled together to form the veins in the plant.

The simple sugar actually helps to create some not-so-simple things. Some of the simple sugar that is made in the leaves provides energy for the plant to grow. Some of it is stored as a starch.

Integrating Science with Reading Instruction · 5–6 © 2002 Creative Teaching Press

Starch can be stored in any part of the plant. When an animal or a person eats these plant parts, they are also consuming the extra energy from the starch. For example, when you eat a salad, your body receives energy from the lettuce. The simple sugar can also be changed into fats. Proteins form when minerals that contain nitrogen compounds combine with the sugar. In this way, a green plant can make all of the chemical compounds that it needs to grow and stay healthy. Plants use proteins and fats to create cells for growth and support and to produce seeds and fruits.

The oxygen that plants give off is essential for us to have clean air to breathe. The stomata release oxygen the plant does not need as well as excess water. Plants usually take in more water than they need. They return the extra water to the environment in the form of water vapor. Plants in tropical rain forests release large amounts of water vapor. This release is how a plant "sweats." This process is called transpiration. Specialized cells, called guard cells, surround the stomata. The guard cells control the amount of water vapor that passes out of a plant's leaves. The guard cells keep the stomata wide open, which allows water to freely leave the plant. When the plant does not have enough water, the guard cells close the stomata opening to slow down the evaporation of water.

We could not live without plants because they are the only natural organisms that can undergo this complex energy change known as photosynthesis. Through the process of photosynthesis, plants give us energy and food, replenish the earth's freshwater supply, and promote clean air. Also, researchers have found that by simply adding a few plants to classrooms, offices, and homes, people get sick less often.

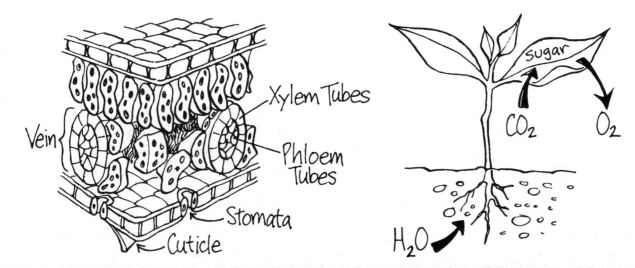

Integrating Science with Reading Instruction · 5–6 © 2002 Creative Teaching Press

Comprehension Questions

Literal Questions

❶ What does the word "photosynthesis" mean?

❷ What are the four elements that must be present in order for photosynthesis to occur?

❸ What is transpiration?

❹ What are the "down elevators"? What do they do?

❺ What role do the stomata play in photosynthesis?

Inferential Questions

❶ Draw a diagram that illustrates the process of photosynthesis. Label the parts of your diagram.

❷ How does photosynthesis affect all living things?

❸ What is the relationship between light and photosynthesis?

❹ How does photosynthesis provide energy to animals and people?

❺ Explain what would happen if one of the elements required for photosynthesis to occur was not present.

Making Connections

❶ Have you ever seen an atrium or a terrarium? How does a terrarium aid the photosynthesis process?

❷ What plants do you have around you? What effect do they have on your environment?

❸ Samuel lives in a city that is often referred to as a "concrete jungle" because there are so many tall buildings and cement walkways but not many trees. Alexis lives in the country with tall trees, lots of grass, hills, and many plants. Based on what you learned from the story, how do you think Alexis and Samuel's lives are different? Why?

❹ What do you notice about how you breathe when you are inside compared to being outside?

❺ What would happen if people cut down all of the rain forests in the world? How would that affect your life?

Integrating Science with Reading Instruction · 5–6 © 2002 Creative Teaching Press

Name _____   Date _____

Sharpen Your Skills

1 In the story on photosynthesis, you read about transpiration. Look at the following words: transpiration—transportation—transit—translation.

What do you think the root word "trans" means?
- ○ close
- ○ full of
- ○ state of
- ○ across

2 What type of words are "cell" and "sell"?
- ○ homographs
- ○ homonyms
- ○ homophones
- ○ homogrids

3 How would you split the word "photosynthesis" into syllables?
- ○ phot-o-syn-thesis
- ○ pho-to-syn-the-sis
- ○ phot-o-syn-thes-is
- ○ ph-oto-syn-thesis

4 The first step in photosynthesis is for the chlorophyll to **trap** the sun's energy.

Which word is an antonym for the word "trap"?
- ○ collect
- ○ absorb
- ○ assign
- ○ release

5 Which word would finish this analogy?

Phloem is to **down elevator** as _____ is to **up elevator.**
- ○ xylem
- ○ transpiration
- ○ oxygen
- ○ stomata

6 What would be a good title for the following category of words?

chlorophyll—solar energy—water—carbon dioxide
- ○ Requirements
- ○ Effects
- ○ Results
- ○ Aids

7 What is the superlative form of the word "healthy"?
- ○ healthiest
- ○ health
- ○ healthier
- ○ healthy

Name _____   Date _____

Get Logical

Ms. Reynold's class is divided into teams. Each team will research a science topic and then teach it to the rest of the class. The Red Team is researching and reporting on photosynthesis. The members of the team are Rachel, Brian, Sheila, Tom, and Raymond. Everyone participated in the research and reporting process. Read the clues below to figure out what part of the photosynthesis process each member focused on.

Clues

❶ Raymond did not focus on one of the four required elements for photosynthesis to occur.

❷ Sheila thought that the pigment of plants was interesting.

❸ Tom read to learn more about a gas that is vital for survival of all plants.

❹ Brian did not do any research on liquids or gases.

	Rachel	Brian	Sheila	Tom	Raymond
Xylem					
Energy					
Chlorophyll					
Carbon Dioxide					
Water					

Rachel researched _____.

Brian researched _____.

Sheila researched _____.

Tom researched _____.

Raymond researched _____.

Integrating Science with Reading Instruction · 5–6 © 2002 Creative Teaching Press

Photosynthesis

How can you find evidence of photosynthesis in a plant?

Teacher Background Information

It is estimated that marine and freshwater algae produce 90% of all the photosynthesis in the world. Land plants produce the remaining 10%. Thus, ocean plants produce the majority of the oxygen in the air. However, it is easier for students to observe photosynthesis in land plants. Photosynthesis starts when sunlight is present. Chlorophyll traps the energy of the sun and uses it to split water molecules into hydrogen and oxygen molecules. The combining of carbon dioxide with the released hydrogen can occur without the presence of sunlight. Scientists refer to the two phases of photosynthesis as the light and dark reactions. During the daytime, and even more during periods of darkness, plants also carry on cellular respiration just like animals. This respiration is the process whereby living organisms release the energy stored in food. During respiration, green plants take in oxygen and release carbon dioxide. Some of the carbon dioxide may be kept by the plant and used later for photosynthesis. The main end product of photosynthesis is simple sugar. Simple sugar is made of single molecules of sugar, $C_6H_{12}O_6$. When a few sugar molecules are linked together, complex sugars are formed. Table sugar, called sucrose, is an example of a double sugar (two molecules linked together). If more sugar molecules are linked together, starches are formed. The hands-on experiment allows students to test for the presence of simple sugar in leaves (green onion), stems (celery), roots (carrot), fruits (apple), and seeds (rice).

Remember that sugar can be transported to any part of the plant. If a plant part does not contain much simple sugar, it may have converted the sugar to starch. Benedict's solution is used to test for the presence of simple sugar.

Before students begin this experiment, place a small piece of carrot, celery, green onion, and apple; a pinch of rice; and a pinch of table sugar in each group's test tubes (one sample per test tube). Cover each sample with a small amount of Benedict's solution (available at science supply stores). Handle the solution carefully, and be sure to wear goggles. If you spill any, wipe it up with paper towels, and wash your hands.

Experiment Results

In the experiment, the rice and table sugar contain no simple sugar, and the solution will remain blue. Sometimes the rice may change to a slightly different shade of blue. The apple will turn a reddish-orange and should have the most simple sugar. The students will be surprised to discover that the celery, carrot, and green onion all contain simple sugar. The celery and green onion usually turn green to orange-green. The amount of simple sugar will vary with individual samples. The celery is a plant stem, and the carrot is a plant root. The green part of the green onion is the leaf. The apple is the fruit, and the rice grains are seeds. The rice does not test positive for simple sugar (or perhaps only a trace amount) because almost all of the sugar has been converted into starch.

Integrating Science with Reading Instruction · 5–6 © 2002 Creative Teaching Press

Photosynthesis

How can you find evidence of photosynthesis in a plant?

Procedure

❶ Put on a pair of goggles.

❷ Have the teacher light your alcohol lamp with a match.

❸ Use the test tube holder to grasp one test tube.

❹ Hold the opening of the test tube away from you, and carefully heat it at an angle over the flame of the alcohol lamp. Let the mixture boil for 5 to 10 seconds, while gently shaking the test tube to mix the contents.

❺ Observe any changes in color. Benedict's solution is blue. If the sample contains a very small amount of simple sugar, it will change to a blue-green color. If the sample contains a small to medium amount of simple sugar, it will change to a yellow-green or green color. If the sample contains a lot of simple sugar, it will change to a red-orange color. If the solution stays blue, that means there is no simple sugar.

❻ Repeat steps 3–6 for each sample.

❼ Record your observations on your Results and Conclusions reproducible.

❽ Throw the contents of the test tubes in the trash. Wash the test tubes.

MATERIALS

(per group)
- ✔ goggles
- ✔ small piece of celery, carrot, green onion, and apple; table sugar; and a pinch of rice
- ✔ 6 test tubes
- ✔ Benedict's solution
- ✔ matches
- ✔ test tube rack (or something similar)
- ✔ test tube holder
- ✔ alcohol lamp
- ✔ paper towels

Integrating Science with Reading Instruction · 5–6 © 2002 Creative Teaching Press

Name _____ Date _____

Photosynthesis

How can you find evidence of photosynthesis in a plant?

Results and Conclusions

1 Record your observations in the chart below.

Sample Tested	Color Change Observed	Amount of Simple Sugar
Celery		
Carrot		
Green Onion		
Apple		
Rice		
Table Sugar		

2 Which sample is a plant stem? _____ A root? _____

3 Which sample is actually a plant leaf? _____

4 Which sample is a fruit? _____ Seeds? _____

5 Did any of the samples tested not have any simple sugar? _____
If so, which ones?

_____

What might be the reason?

_____

6 How can you find evidence of photosynthesis in a plant?

_____

Integrating Science with Reading Instruction · 5–6 © 2002 Creative Teaching Press

Catch a Clue

What will we learn about in our reading today?

nutrition

hygiene

weathering

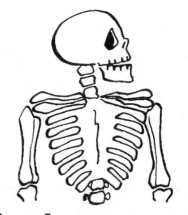

body systems

Our Clues

❶ It is related to human beings.

❷ It does not involve the outside of our bodies.

❸ We will not focus on what we eat.

❹ We will learn about what we have in common.

Concept Map

Facts we already know about **body systems,** and the new facts we have learned

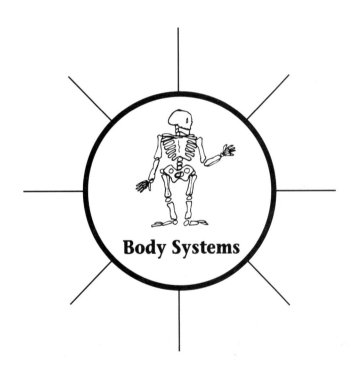

Body Systems

Word Warm-Up

Which words might you expect to find in a story about **body systems?**

spinal cord	waste	voluntary
functions	muscles	telephone
acid	magazine	systems
organs	tissues	digestive

Integrating Science with Reading Instruction · 5–6 © 2002 Creative Teaching Press

Body Systems

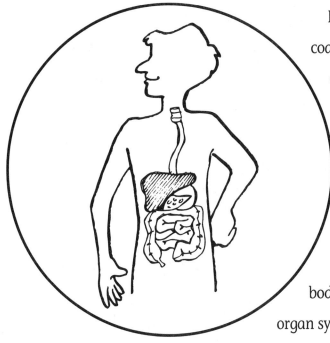

Last week I scored a goal in my soccer game! My coach reminded me that I did not score it all on my own. The goalie first kicked the ball to Jimmy who dribbled it halfway up the field and passed it to Tim. Tim dribbled the ball to the far corner of the field, passed it across to me, and I kicked it in the goal. We were so excited! Because our team worked together, we were able to win the game!

In the same way, the many parts of your body (which is made up of cells, tissues, organs, and organ systems) work together as a "team" to perform bodily functions. When many organs work together, they form an "organ system." There are nine organ systems in your body. They are the skeletal, respiratory, nervous, muscular, digestive, circulatory, excretory, endocrine, and reproductive systems.

Did you know that without your skeletal system, you would be like a blob of Jell-O® on the floor? Your skeletal system holds up your body, allows you to move, and protects your vital organs such as your heart, lungs, and brain. It includes your bones, joints, cartilage, and ligaments.

Take a deep breath and let it out. You can thank your respiratory system for that! When you inhaled, you took in the oxygen from the air. When you exhaled, you got rid of the carbon dioxide that you did not need. The "team players" that help you to breathe are your mouth, your windpipe, your lungs, a muscle that controls your breathing, two tubes that carry air to your lungs, and smaller tubes and tiny air sacs inside of your lungs.

Can you guess which organ system is the most complex and fragile? If you guessed your nervous system, you are right! This system includes your brain, your spinal cord, and all your nerves. Your spinal cord receives messages from your brain and sends them to the other parts of your body. Everything that you see, hear, smell, taste, or touch becomes a message and is sent to the spinal cord and brain to be read. Then, your brain can send back an answer to your muscles, organs, and glands.

Integrating Science with Reading Instruction · 5–6 © 2002 Creative Teaching Press

Sometimes, your spinal cord recognizes a familiar message and will send an answer back right away without sending the message to your brain first. This is called a reflex. Your body responds so quickly because it does not need to think about it. This is why you automatically blink when something is coming right at your face.

Have you ever had goose bumps when you were cold? Did you know your muscular system causes the goose bumps? Your muscular system includes two kinds of muscles. There are voluntary and involuntary muscles. Voluntary muscles cover the skeleton and are controlled by what you are thinking. Your lip muscles are an example of voluntary muscles. If your teacher asks you to stop talking, you CAN stop because you tell yourself to stop moving those muscles. Involuntary muscles are the opposite. If they are healthy, they work whether or not you are thinking about them. Your heart is an example of an involuntary muscle. It pumps blood even when you are not thinking about it. There are tiny involuntary muscles in your skin that give you goose bumps when you are cold.

Another organ system in your body is the digestive system. The food we eat needs to be broken down before our body can absorb or eliminate it. Your teeth, tongue, and saliva break down food. After you swallow it, the food is sent down your esophagus into your stomach. When the food reaches your stomach, acid breaks down the food even more. After it passes through your small intestine, the digestive process is complete. Then, the body can absorb the nutrients it needs, and the excretory system removes and eliminates wastes from the body.

The circulatory system uses your heart, arteries, veins, capillaries, and blood. Your heart pumps blood to the rest of your body through arteries, which then divide into small capillaries. Veins return blood to your heart. Your endocrine system is made of glands that produce hormones to regulate your growth and development. Your reproductive system makes it possible for you to have babies when you are older. As you can see, the human body is a complex "team" where every "player" relies on the others to do their jobs.

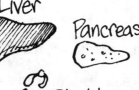

Integrating Science with Reading Instruction · 5–6 © 2002 Creative Teaching Press

Comprehension Questions

Integrating Science with Reading Instruction · 5–6 © 2002 Creative Teaching Press

Literal Questions

❶ What is formed when many organs in your body work together?

❷ What are your nine organ systems? List two characteristics of each system.

❸ Which organ system is the most complex and fragile?

❹ What are the different types of muscles in your body? Give two examples of each type.

❺ Explain why you automatically blink when something is coming at your face.

Inferential Questions

❶ How does blood flow through your body? Clearly explain the flow and identify the organ system that is responsible.

❷ Which organ system is affected when people have asthma? What effect do you think an inhaler has?

❸ Pretend that you just ate a candy bar. Explain in detail what happened to the candy bar. Use the language you learned from the story in your explanation.

❹ When the doctor checks the reflexes in your knee, are you using voluntary or involuntary muscles?

❺ Why is oxygen important to your life?

Making Connections

❶ Choose one organ system. Create a commercial or advertisement to tell everyone how important that organ system is.

❷ Rank the organ systems that you read about according to how much you already knew about them. Next to each system, list a new fact that you learned.

❸ Some people have disabilities that make them shake, tremble, or nod uncontrollably. What is really going on? People often make fun of others who make unusual involuntary movements. Is this fair? Why or why not?

❹ In the story of *The Three Little Pigs*, the Big Bad Wolf used one of his organ systems repeatedly. Which organ system did he use? How did he use it?

❺ Athletes go to extra measures to keep their organ systems in "top-notch" condition. Name at least one thing that athletes might do to enhance the performance of each organ system.

Sharpen Your Skills

1 The heart pumps blood throughout your body.

In which of these sentences is the division of the subject and the predicate shown properly?

○ The heart / pumps blood throughout your body.
○ The heart pumps blood / throughout your body.
○ The heart pumps / blood throughout your body.
○ The heart pumps blood throughout / your body.

2 Every organ system is **vital** to your survival.

What does the word "vital" mean?

○ important ○ unique
○ beneficial ○ necessary

3 The doctors were optimistic that the heart transplant would be successful for the ailing patient.

What is the meaning of this sentence?

○ They hope he gets better.
○ They think he will be healthy once again.
○ They hope the heart transplant works.
○ They predict that their surgery will help him.

4 If you wanted to find the pronunciation of the word "excretory," which resource would be the most helpful?

○ dictionary ○ atlas
○ almanac ○ thesaurus

5 The respiratory therapist needed a lung transplant.

This sentence is an example of _____.

○ humor ○ irony
○ alliteration ○ metaphor

6 Which term would finish this analogy?

Excretory system is to **eliminate waste** as _____ is to **allow movement**.

○ muscular system ○ digestive system
○ circulatory system ○ reproductive system

7 What is missing from the following classification sequence?

cells _____ organs organ systems

○ systems ○ atoms
○ tissues ○ organisms

Integrating Science with Reading Instruction · 5–6 © 2002 Creative Teaching Press

Name _____   Date _____

Harbor View General Hospital has just hired five new doctors: Dr. Able, Dr. Help, Dr. Better, Dr. Care, and Dr. Love. Each doctor specializes in one of the following areas of medicine: respiratory care, digestive disorders, heart surgery, bones and joints, and brain surgery. Use the clues below to decide which area of medicine each doctor specializes in.

Clues

❶ Dr. Better does not perform surgery. Instead, he helps people with esophageal and stomach problems.

❷ Dr. Able is a surgeon.

❸ Most of Dr. Care's patients are referred to her after they fall down in some way.

❹ Dr. Love does not help people with respiratory problems or heart problems.

❺ Dr. Help helps people breathe a little easier.

	Dr. Able	Dr. Help	Dr. Better	Dr. Care	Dr. Love
Respiratory Care					
Digestive Disorders					
Heart Surgery					
Bones and Joints					
Brain Surgery					

Integrating Science with Reading Instruction · 5–6 © 2002 Creative Teaching Press

Dr. Able specializes in _____.

Dr. Help specializes in _____.

Dr. Better specializes in _____.

Dr. Care specializes in _____.

Dr. Love specializes in _____.

Body Systems

How does your diaphragm help you breathe?

Teacher Background Information

The act of breathing involves more than just your lungs, which are composed of millions of tiny air sacs called alveoli. A good analogy would be to compare the lungs to large clusters of tiny grapes. Each grape represents one air sac (alveolus). Several changes take place to force air in and out of the lungs. The ribs move up and outward, and the diaphragm moves down, making the chest cavity larger. As a result, there is less air pressure inside the lungs. The greater air pressure outside of the body pushes air into the lungs. When you exhale, the reverse occurs. The rib cage drops down and inward, and the diaphragm moves upward towards the lungs, making the space inside the chest cavity smaller, increasing the air pressure within the lungs. The greater air pressure forces air out of the lungs.

In this experiment, students construct a working model of the main parts of their respiratory system. You will need to punch a hole in the bottom of a plastic cup for each student. It is easy to prepare the cups if you heat up an ice pick or old meat thermometer and gently let the tip melt through the bottom of each cup. The hole should be just big enough to fit a straw through it. This project takes about 1 hour to complete, plus additional time to answer questions. It can be spread over two periods of time. The process can be sped up if you help students apply the rubber cement in step 5. Have students check to see if their "lungs" (small balloons) work properly. Have them remove the straw from the cup, and gently suck in on the end of the "Y" straw, and then release the air. The small balloons (lungs) should collapse and then inflate a little. Students can make any changes or repairs, if needed, at this time. If necessary, you can have students stop after step 5 and continue the rest of the experiment at a later time.

Experiment Results

The plastic cup represents the chest cavity with the rib cage. The longer piece of straw is the windpipe, or trachea. The Y-shaped straw pieces represent the bronchial tubes, and the small balloons represent the lungs. The students should be aware that the lungs do not look like one big empty balloon in real life, but instead are made of many tiny air sacs (alveoli), which look more like large clusters of grapes. The large balloon functions as the diaphragm. When students gently pull down on the diaphragm balloon, the lungs (small balloons) will inflate (inhale). This happens due to the difference in air pressure, with the pressure being greater outside the lungs, which forces air into the lungs. When students release the balloon diaphragm, the lungs will deflate (exhale). Again, this is because of the difference in air pressure. The increased air pressure within the lungs (as compared to outside the body) forces the air out of the lungs.

Integrating Science with Reading Instruction · 5–6 © 2002 Creative Teaching Press

Body Systems

How does your diaphragm help you breathe?

Procedure

1 Stretch the ribbed section of the 2" flexible straw open. Use the hole punch to make a hole *in the middle of half of the ribbed section* of the straw. (Note: Only go partway through the straw. It should look like a "bite" was taken out of the straw.) Push the straw ends back together to close the ribbed section.

2 Apply rubber cement around each end of the small straw. (Do not glue the straw opening closed.) Slide a small empty water balloon onto each end of the straw. Set aside the straw to dry. Turn your cup upside down on a table.

3 Use the scissors to cut one end of the larger straw (3" piece of straw) into a point. This will form two prongs.

4 Bend the small straw into a "V," and insert the prongs of the pointed straw into the hole at the top of the "V."

5 Ask a classmate to apply rubber cement around the base of the "V" shape while you push the two straw pieces together. Gently blow on it to help it dry a little faster. Insert the straw into the hole in the plastic cup in a "Y" position. Let it dry. Now help your partner complete this step.

6 Remove the straw from its drying position, and insert it into the cup in an upside down "Y" position. Put rubber cement around the straw where it comes out of the cup. Let it dry while you complete step 7.

7 Blow up the large balloon, and quietly let the air out three times. (This is to stretch the balloon.) Cut off the top one-third of the balloon. (Cut off all of the neck and a little of the round, fatter part.)

8 Firmly hold the cup at the bottom with the cup opening facing up. Work with your partner to stretch the large balloon over the opening of the cup. (Pull it about 1/4" or 6.4 mm over the edge of the cup.) Use a permanent marker to write your name on the edge of the balloon. Gently pinch the large balloon, slightly pull down on it (about 1" or 2.5 cm), and then let go. Observe what happens.

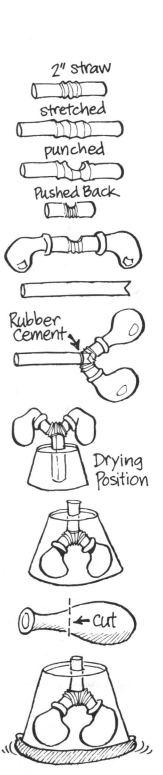

2" straw

stretched

punched

Pushed Back

Rubber Cement

Drying Position

← cut

Name _____   Date _____

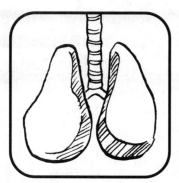

Body Systems

How does your diaphragm help you breathe?

Results and Conclusions

1 What part of your respiratory system does the plastic cup represent?

_____

2 What does the longer piece of straw represent?

_____

3 What do the small Y-shaped straw pieces represent?

_____

4 What do the small balloons represent?

_____

Is this what these organs really look like in your body?

_____

5 What does the large balloon represent?

_____

6 What happened when you gently pulled down on the large balloon?

_____

Why did this happen?

_____

7 What happened when you released the large balloon?

_____

Why did this happen?

_____

8 How does your diaphragm help you breathe?

_____

Integrating Science with Reading Instruction · 5–6 © 2002 Creative Teaching Press

Catch a Clue

What will we learn about in our reading today?

the planet Earth

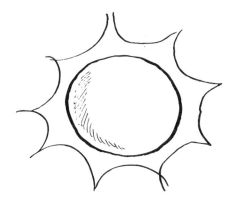

our Sun

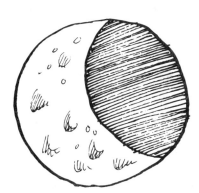

our Moon

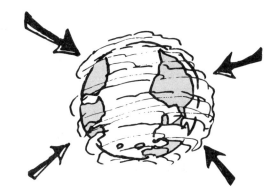

our atmosphere

Our Clues

1 It is in the area of scientific research called astronomy.

2 You can see it from Earth.

3 It rotates and revolves.

4 It reflects light.

Concept Map

Facts we already know about **the phases of the Moon,** and the new facts we have learned

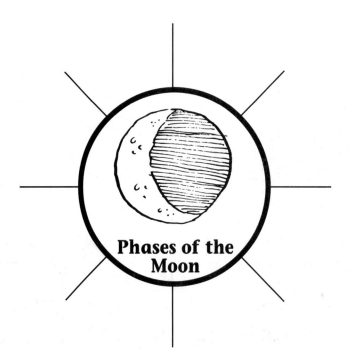

Phases of the Moon

Integrating Science with Reading Instruction · 5–6 © 2002 Creative Teaching Press

Word Warm-Up

 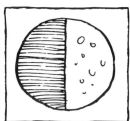  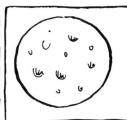

Which words might you expect to find in a story about **phases of the Moon?**

eclipse	phases	cookies
reflection	quarter	waning
lunar	bicycle	waxing
calendar	shadow	revolve

Phases of the Moon

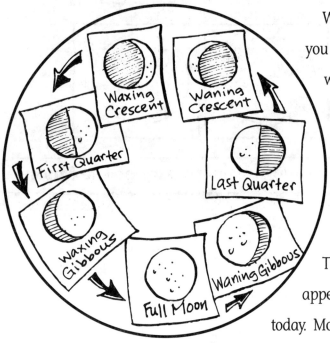

What do you see when you look at the Moon? Do you see a man in the Moon? Some people think that what they see looks like a man's face. What they are noticing are the light and dark patches of the Moon. Scientists used to think that the dark patches were filled with water and named them seas. After astronauts visited the Moon, we discovered that there is no water on the Moon. These dark areas are just lower, flat plains that appear in shadow. However, they are still called seas today. Mountains and craters surround some of these dark areas. That is what makes some people think they see a man's face.

Maybe you have noticed that on some nights there is a full moon and on other nights you can only see a sliver of it. What happened? The different shapes of the Moon are related to the positions of the Moon, the Earth, and the Sun. The Moon does not produce any of its own light. What you are really seeing is the reflection of the Sun's light. It takes the Moon about one month to revolve around the Earth. At the same time, the Moon is rotating, or turning around. Throughout the month, you will notice that the portion of the Moon that is lit up changes the shape of the Moon in the sky. These changes are called the Moon's phases.

Let's begin on a cloudless night when you cannot see the Moon. This phase is called a new moon. This occurs when the Moon is between the Earth and the Sun. The side of the Moon that is not lit up by the Sun faces the Earth at this time. This makes the Moon look dark. Sometimes, we can see a faint outline of the new moon. This is caused by sunlight that is reflected from the Earth back to the Moon. However, most of the time we do not see anything when there is a new moon. A few days later, you would see a crescent moon. By the end of the week, you would see half of the Moon's surface lit up. This is called a quarter moon. A few days later, you could see an area of the Moon's surface that is larger than half of the Moon but less than a full moon. This is called a gibbous moon. Two weeks into

Integrating Science with Reading Instruction · 5–6 © 2002 Creative Teaching Press

the cycle you would see a full moon. A full moon occurs when the Earth is between the Moon and the Sun. These are the brightest nights of the month. These nights you can walk outside in most areas and see in front of you without using a flashlight! Waxing is when the lit portion of the Moon is growing. Waxing means appearing. A few days after the full moon, we would see the Moon's lit portion decrease. This forms a gibbous moon again. A week later, we would see a quarter moon again. Finally, at the end of the month, we would see a new moon again. Waning is when the lit portion of the Moon is shrinking. Waning means going away. Wow! You can see so many interesting changes in the night sky throughout the month!

The Moon's phases take place in a lunar month (lunar means moon). This is shorter than a month on our calendar. So, every couple of years there will actually be two full moons in one month. This is called a blue moon. Some calendars list the phases of the Moon so you can observe them. You can also get that information in a daily newspaper or on the Internet.

Sometimes when the Earth passes between the Sun and the Moon, the Earth blocks the Sun's light. This creates a shadow over the Moon. When this happens, we cannot see the Moon. This is called a lunar eclipse. This occurs only at the time of a full moon. In a solar eclipse (solar means sun), the Moon passes between the Earth and the Sun and blocks the light of the Sun from hitting Earth for a short time. The Moon's shadow falls on the Earth. A solar eclipse only occurs at the time of a new moon.

Now you are ready to go out and observe the Moon. You do not even need a telescope. You will now be able to identify which phase of the Moon is in the sky on almost any night. You can check to see if your prediction for the next night is correct by looking in your newspaper or on the Internet. If all of this fascinates you and you would like to look at patterns of the Moon's phases from the past, you can look in an almanac. If you are more interested in observations, lunar activity, eclipses, and the phases of the Moon, then one day you might want to become an astronomer.

Integrating Science with Reading Instruction · 5–6 © 2002 Creative Teaching Press

Comprehension Questions

? Literal Questions

❶ What is a lunar eclipse? How is it different from a solar eclipse?

❷ What is on the surface of the Moon? What can we see from Earth?

❸ What are the phases of the Moon? Why do they change?

❹ What resources could you look at to find out what phase the Moon will be in tonight? Where could you find out what the phase of the Moon was on that same date last year?

❺ What do we call the phases of the Moon in which part is appearing or disappearing?

? Inferential Questions

❶ What mistake did scientists make years ago, which is a bit misleading today?

❷ Why do we think we see images of a man's face when we look at the Moon?

❸ Why don't we have eclipses more often?

❹ Why do calendars list the phases of the Moon?

❺ If there was a full moon last night, when do you predict you will see a gibbous moon?

? Making Connections

❶ What can you see on the surface of the Moon without looking through a telescope? If you had a telescope, what difference would it make?

❷ Why is it important for you to learn about the phases of the Moon and why they change over time?

❸ Would you ever want to travel into space and land on the Moon? Why or why not? What would you expect to see? How would you prepare for the trip? What materials would you need?

❹ Astronomers make predictions, test their predictions through investigations, and then prove or disprove them. You read about a prediction that was made years ago, which has since been disproven. How are you like an astronomer in the sense that you have thought something would happen or was true, but you later found out that it wasn't?

❺ Create a diagram or mobile to illustrate the phases of the Moon.

Integrating Science with Reading Instruction · 5–6 © 2002 Creative Teaching Press

Sharpen Your Skills

1 The camp seemed as far away as the Moon.

This sentence used _____ language.

○ literal   ○ interpretive

○ figurative   ○ abstract

2 Don't worry. I can carry the tent all by myself because it is so **light.** I do not even need a lantern, since it is so **light** outside.

In these sentences, the word "light" is used as a _____.

○ homonym   ○ homophone

○ synonym   ○ simile

3 The Earth blocks the Sun's light and creates a shadow over the Moon.

What does the word "blocks" mean?

○ covers   ○ stands in the way of

○ made of wood   ○ highlights

4 What is missing from the following sequence?

crescent   quarter   _____   full

○ waxing gibbous   ○ new moon

○ waning gibbous   ○ crescent

5 Which word would finish this analogy?

Waxing is to **appearing** as _____ is to **disappearing.**

○ invisible   ○ gibbous

○ waning   ○ wandering

6 Look at the list of types of moons: waning gibbous—crescent moon—waxing gibbous—new moon.

Which type of moon does not belong with the others?

○ waning gibbous   ○ crescent moon

○ waxing gibbous   ○ new moon

7 If you wanted to learn more about the lunar month or the Moon itself, which resource would be the most helpful?

○ dictionary   ○ encyclopedia

○ atlas   ○ thesaurus

Integrating Science with Reading Instruction · 5-6 © 2002 Creative Teaching Press

Get Logical

Last February, five different students in Mrs. Aguilar's class recorded the phases of the Moon. Each student was responsible for observing the Moon each night and watching for a particular phase. Every time students saw the Moon in their assigned phase, they recorded it in a notebook and on a chart at school. Sylvia, Courtney, Emily, Dylan, and Tobias participated in this project. The Moon phases they recorded included full moon, new moon, gibbous moon, waxing moon, and waning moon. Use the clues below to decide who recorded which phase of the Moon.

Clues

1 Dylan saw either all of the Moon or none of the Moon.

2 Courtney saw almost three-quarters of the Moon lit up.

3 The night was so bright on the night that Tobias recorded his observations. Wow!

4 Emily recorded her observations as the Moon was disappearing in the night sky and before Dylan recorded his observations.

5 Sylvia did not observe a full moon or a new moon on her observation nights.

	Sylvia	Courtney	Emily	Dylan	Tobias
Full Moon					
New Moon					
Gibbous Moon					
Waxing Moon					
Waning Moon					

Sylvia recorded the _____ phase.

Courtney recorded the _____ phase.

Emily recorded the _____ phase.

Dylan recorded the _____ phase.

Tobias recorded the _____ phase.

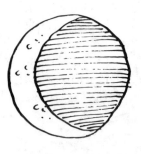

Integrating Science with Reading Instruction · 5–6 © 2002 Creative Teaching Press

Phases of the Moon

How does the Moon travel in space, and how does this movement cause a full moon and a new moon?

Teacher Background Information

The Moon revolves around the Earth every month, or every 29½ days to be exact. The Moon takes just as long to rotate as it does to revolve. This means that the Moon has about two weeks of daylight and then two weeks of darkness each month. From our perspective here on Earth, the Moon does not seem to rotate. That is because whenever we look up at the Moon we always see the same side. Only from outer space can you actually tell that the Moon is rotating. The Moon's orbit is slightly tilted and is not in straight alignment with the Earth. We can see the side of the Moon early in the morning, late in the afternoon, and during the night. This is because the Sun's rays are very bright during the middle portion of the day and because the Earth's atmosphere scatters the sunlight in all directions. As the Moon travels around the Earth, we see different amounts of its lighted surface. The changes in the Moon's appearance are called the phases of the Moon. Before the hands-on experiment, paint a Styrofoam ball for each pair of students. Use black acrylic paint to paint half of each ball. When the paint is dry, carefully put a bamboo skewer into each ball where the black and white halves meet.

Experiment Results

It will be obvious to the students that the teacher "Moon" revolved around the student "Earth." The Moon did not appear to rotate at first. The Earth person does see something different from the rest of the class. From the perspective of being on the Earth, we can only see one side of the Moon. Only the rest of the class (the space aliens) could actually "see" that the Moon did rotate. The students should learn that it takes the Moon just as long to rotate as it does to revolve. The illustration that shows the Earth between the Sun and the Moon is the correct position for a full moon. The sunlight can shine on the full half of the Moon that we can see, and yet it is dark (nighttime) on our side of the Earth. The illustration that shows the Moon between the Earth and the Sun is the correct position for a new moon. The side of the Moon that is not illuminated is facing the Earth. When we have an eclipse, the Sun, the Moon, and the Earth are more in a straight alignment, the light behind the Moon and Earth is blocked. The Earth blocks the light of the Sun from hitting the Moon during a lunar eclipse. The Moon blocks the Sun's light from falling on the Earth during a solar eclipse. Explain that the reason it looks so confusing is that it takes the Moon just as long to rotate as it does to revolve and that is why people on the Earth only see one side of the Moon. You can act this out again, if necessary. Give a copy of the procedure for the experiment to each student *after* you do the teacher demonstration with the whole class.

Phases of the Moon

How does the Moon travel in space, and how does this movement cause a full moon and a new moon?

Procedure

Teacher Demonstration for Students

1 Ask a student to stand in front of the class to represent the Earth. Ask the "Earth" (student volunteer) to rotate (turn around) slowly. Explain that you (the teacher) will be the "Moon." Slowly move around the Earth, always facing the student as you move sideways around him or her. (At first glance, you will not appear to have rotated.) Ask the volunteer if he or she saw you (the Moon) **revolve** around the Earth. (Yes) Ask the "space aliens" (the rest of the class) if they saw the Moon revolve. (Yes)

2 Then, ask the Earth and the space aliens if they saw the Moon **rotate.** (Generally, they will both say no.) Tell the Earth and space aliens that if you rotated they should see the front of you, the side of you, the back of you, the other side, and then the front of you again.

3 Act out the demonstration again. Ask the Earth student again if he or she saw all sides of you. He or she will say no. Ask the class if they saw all sides of you. (They will now answer yes.)

Student Experiment

1 Take turns with your partner holding the Styrofoam model of the Moon. Pretend your eyes are the people on the Earth.

2 Make a fist with your other hand. Pretend this is the Sun. Can you represent a full moon? Where would you put the Moon and your fist (the Sun)?

3 Try to represent a new moon. Where would you put the Moon and your fist (the Sun)?

4 Think about how an eclipse might occur.

Integrating Science with Reading Instruction · 5–6 © 2002 Creative Teaching Press

Name _____   Date _____

Phases of the Moon

How does the Moon travel in space, and how does this movement cause a full moon and a new moon?

Results and Conclusions

1 Did your teacher (the "Moon") appear to revolve around the Earth?

_____

2 Did the Moon appear to the "space alien" students to rotate? _____ Why or why not?

_____

3 Did the "Earth" student see something different than the rest of the class? _____ Why or why not?

_____

4 Explain what you learned about how the Moon moves around the Earth.

_____

5 What are the relative positions of the Earth, Moon, and Sun when we see a full moon?

_____

6 What are the relative positions of the Earth, Moon, and Sun when we have a new moon?

_____

7 What do you think happens when we have an eclipse?

_____

8 How does the Moon travel in space, and how does this movement cause a full moon and a new moon?

_____

Integrating Science with Reading Instruction · 5–6 © 2002 Creative Teaching Press

Catch a Clue

the human skeleton

outer space

volcanic activity

ecosystems

Our Clues

1 It is not related to individual people.

2 Our Earth is an important factor.

3 It involves many different types of matter and material.

4 It is out of our range of vision.

Integrating Science with Reading Instruction · 5–6 © 2002 Creative Teaching Press

Concept Map

Facts we already know about **outer space,** and the new facts we have learned

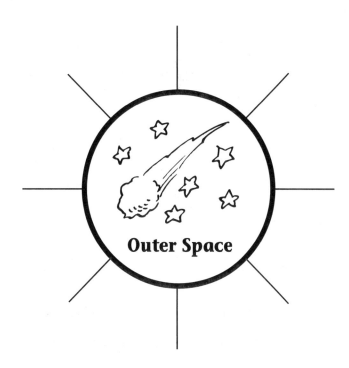

Outer Space

Word Warm-Up

Which words might you expect to find in a story about **outer space?**

galaxies	sand	astronomers
universe	immense	Frisbee®
bodies	meteors	gases
telescope	constellations	particles

Integrating Science with Reading Instruction · 5–6 © 2002 Creative Teaching Press

Outer Space

Have you ever wondered what is really in outer space? What exactly is the universe? The word universe is used to refer to all of outer space. Astronomers have studied space for many years, but they still have more questions than answers. No one knows just how large our universe really is. We do know that the universe is immense and the distances between objects are tremendous. But how far is "far away"? Let's give it a try. Imagine that the distance between the Sun and the Earth is equal to the size of one grain of sand. Using this size as a comparison, then the dwarf planet we call Pluto would be 30 feet (9.15 m) away. The closest star beyond the Sun, called Alpha Centauri, would be 50 miles (80.5 km) away. This makes it easier to understand just how far away things in outer space really are.

However, astronomers prefer to use the term "light-years" to measure distances from Earth. A light-year describes how far light can travel in one year. Astronomers chose light as a reference point because it travels faster than anything else does. In fact, if you shined a beam of light all the way around the world, it could go around $7\frac{1}{2}$ times in one second! Now that is speedy traveling! Scientists guess that the universe is at least 10 billion light-years across, and it seems to be getting larger.

The universe is made up of a lot of empty space. Huge swirling masses of stars, called galaxies, are scattered throughout the universe. Each galaxy is made of billions of stars. Our solar system can be found within a galaxy, called the Milky Way. The Milky Way has a shape similar to a spinning Frisbee® but with a bigger bulge in the middle. Our solar system would be located out on one side of the Frisbee.

There are many different kinds of stars, some old and some new. Some stars are brighter than others. Stars that are the hottest appear white through a telescope. Stars that are not quite as hot appear yellow, like our Sun. Those stars that are even cooler will appear red in color. Stars are born,

Integrating Science with Reading Instruction · 5–6 © 2002 Creative Teaching Press

grow older, and then die. They are constantly repeating this life cycle, even though they are not really alive. Have you ever looked for the Big Dipper or the Little Dipper in the sky at night? If you have, then you have looked for constellations. Constellations are patterns of stars that form a specific shape in the sky.

In between the stars, there are cloud-like shapes of gases and dust called nebulae. A single nebula can have almost any shape. Some nebulae do not give off any light. We can see some of them because they reflect the light of nearby stars. A star is born when the gases in these clouds condense enough for nuclear reactions to begin. A star is like a nuclear bomb inside of a very strong box. Instead of exploding all at once, imagine the box opening and closing, releasing the bomb's energy a little bit at a time, over a long period of time. That is what a star does. A star will continue to burn up its gases and give off heat and light for billions of years. It may end its life quietly by becoming a black dwarf (a very small star that emits no visible light) when it can no longer shine. Or, it may end in a supernova explosion (a very big, bright explosion).

In addition to planets and moons in our solar system, there are bodies known as comets, asteroids, and meteors. Comets are like dirty snowballs made of frozen gases, dust, and rock particles. They travel in long oblong orbits around the Sun. As they get closer to the Sun they become warmer and begin to melt. Sometimes a gas "tail" is formed from the melted gases. If you looked at a comet through a telescope, it would look like a fuzzy head with a long tail. You may have heard of Halley's Comet. This comet was named after Edmund Halley who predicted it would return. Maybe some day you could have a comet named after you!

Asteroids and meteors are also found in space. These are really just pieces of space "junk." They are made of bits of rock and metal. Asteroids are quite large and meteors are smaller. A meteor that enters the Earth's atmosphere at a high speed usually burns up. This kind of meteor is called a shooting star even though it is not really a star. It is called a meteorite if it lands on the ground.

Now you know the universe is enormous! It includes billions of galaxies, planets, moons, stars, meteors, comets, and so much more that is yet to be discovered. Astronomers will understand more about how stars are formed and how huge our universe really is one day. For now, we can all observe some of the amazing characteristics of outer space each night and leave the rest up to our imaginations and the scientists!

Integrating Science with Reading Instruction · 5–6 © 2002 Creative Teaching Press

Comprehension Questions

Literal Questions

1. How big is our universe? Discuss the frame of reference presented in the story.
2. What is in our universe? Be specific.
3. What is the difference between asteroids and meteors?
4. What are the groups of stars in the sky called? What are some examples? What is a "shooting star"?
5. Who predicted the return of a comet? What was that comet called? Why?

Inferential Questions

1. Astronomers have been studying the universe for many years. Why don't astronomers know more about our universe if they have been studying it for so long?
2. Why do you think some stars are brighter than others?
3. How are stars born? What happens when they die?
4. What do you think the difference is between a black dwarf and a supernova explosion?
5. Why is it that you see shooting stars on some nights but not on others?

Making Connections

1. Have you ever looked through a telescope? If so, what have you seen? If not, what would you expect to see?
2. Describe the similarities between the "life span" of a star and a person.
3. Why don't we have a space museum that displays examples of meteorites, asteroids, nebulae, and other pieces of distant solar systems?
4. If you were to become an astronomer's assistant for one day, what would you want to learn more about as it relates to our universe?
5. Many space movies have been made that involve aliens, spaceships landing on other planets, what is visible from space, and other galaxies. What is reality and what is fantasy? Do you think that anything we think is fantasy today could be discovered as reality tomorrow? Why?

Sharpen Your Skills

1 The **remains** of the exploded star may be scattered into outer space, providing material for new nebulae to form.

What does the word "remains" mean?
- ○ material left over
- ○ answer
- ○ dissolved particles
- ○ space material

2 If you wanted to learn more about outer space, what resource would be the most helpful?
- ○ dictionary
- ○ atlas
- ○ Internet
- ○ almanac

3 The collapsed remains of this very large star are now so **densely** held together than not even light can escape from it.

Which word is a synonym for the word "densely"?
- ○ loosely
- ○ cleverly
- ○ quickly
- ○ tightly

4 The tail of a comet always faces away from the Sun **since** it is being blown back from the head by the Sun.

In this sentence, what part of speech is the word "since"?
- ○ adjective
- ○ adverb
- ○ preposition
- ○ conjunction

5 What is missing from the following sequence?

Earth   _____   Milky Way Galaxy   universe
- ○ solar system
- ○ Neptune
- ○ Mars
- ○ Big Dipper

6 Which word would finish this analogy?

Scale is to **weight** as _____ are to **distance in space.**
- ○ miles
- ○ constellations
- ○ light-years
- ○ grains of sand

7 Look at the following words: astronomy—astrology—astronaut.

What do you think the root word "astro" means?
- ○ wind
- ○ Earth
- ○ star
- ○ science

Integrating Science with Reading Instruction · 5–6 © 2002 Creative Teaching Press

Name _____   Date _____

Get Logical

At NASA, five astronomers are doing five different experiments with new telescopes to learn more about the world beyond our own. Luke, Walker, Obie, Dewey, and Hailey are each conducting an experiment. Their experiments involve learning about galaxies, comets, stars, planets, and nebulae. Use the clues below to decide what each astronomer investigated.

Clues

❶ Walker focused on huge swirling masses of stars scattered throughout the universe.
❷ Hailey did not conduct any experiment related to stars, comets, or clouds of gases.
❸ The experiment that Obie conducted examined how temperature affects the color of what he was investigating.
❹ When it was Dewey's turn to share, he showed us a picture that looked like a fuzzy head with a tail!
❺ Luke conducted the experiment on gases that could take on any shape in space.

	Luke	Walker	Obie	Dewey	Hailey
Galaxies					
Comets					
Stars					
Planets					
Nebulae					

Luke investigated _____.
Walker investigated _____.
Obie investigated _____.
Dewey investigated _____.
Hailey investigated _____.

Spiral Galaxy

Integrating Science with Reading Instruction · 5–6 © 2002 Creative Teaching Press

Outer Space

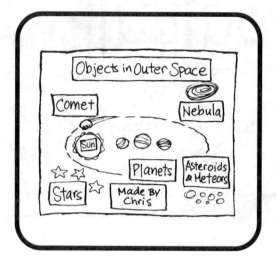

What kinds of objects, aside from planets, are found in our solar system and beyond?

Teacher Background Information

It is important for students to understand that there is a lot more in outer space than just the planets within our solar system. In addition to the planets and their moons, our solar system has bodies known as comets, asteroids, and meteors. Comets travel in long oval-shaped orbits. This brings them close to the Sun part of the time, and then sends them very far out into the solar system. That is why we do not see comets all the time. They are only visible when their oblong orbit brings them closer to the Sun and the Earth. If a comet has a tail, it only forms when the comet is closer to the Sun. The tail is created when a little of the comet's "head" melts, vaporizes, and trails behind. A comet's tail always faces away from the Sun, so it changes its position as it travels. Asteroids and meteors are really pieces of space junk, made of rock and metal. Asteroids are quite large, while meteors are smaller. Most of outer space is just empty space. Of the many stars that we see in the sky at night, some are part of our Milky Way Galaxy, while others are actually much farther away in space. Constellations are just "star pictures" that people imagined they saw in the sky many years ago. The stars seem to twinkle when we look at them. However, they really do not. It is just the action of the light passing through the Earth's atmosphere that makes them appear to twinkle. If you viewed the stars from outer space, they would shine continuously.

When students make their asteroids and meteors, using the top from a box that holds ten reams of copy paper works well to hold the vermiculite, and it avoids "meteor showers" in the classroom. You can make a cardboard pattern for the comet's oblong orbit if you wish, or have students draw freehand. Vermiculite can be bought from a garden shop.

Experiment Results

In constructing this project, students should gain an understanding that there are a lot of things in outer space besides our Sun and the planets of our solar system. Hopefully, they will also appreciate how small our portion of outer space is. Black construction paper is used because most of outer space is dark and black. Asteroids and meteors are both pieces of space junk (made of rock and metal); however, asteroids are much larger than meteors. Nebulae are clouds in outer space, and the chalk smudge gives a "cloudy" appearance. Nebulae are not pinpoints of light, the way most stars appear. Most nebulae are just irregular shapes of dust and gases. The main difference between a comet's orbit and a planet's orbit is that the ends of a comet's orbit are not equidistant from the Sun. The orbit is very oblong (planetary orbits are only slightly elliptical), and one end of the comet's orbit is close to the Sun while the other end is far away from the Sun.

Integrating Science with Reading Instruction · 5–6 © 2002 Creative Teaching Press

Outer Space

What kinds of objects, aside from planets, are found in our solar system and beyond?

Procedure

1 Cover the tables with newspaper. Give one piece of black construction paper to each student.

2 Dip a toothbrush into the white paint. Wipe off the extra paint on the side of the cup. Hold the toothbrush bristle side down. Rub <u>one</u> finger over the toothbrush bristles to splatter paint to create a white starry background on the black paper. Let the paint dry for a few minutes.

3 Meanwhile, pick at least three of your favorite planets, color them and the Sun, and then cut them out.

4 Cut out the title and labels. Glue the "Objects in Outer Space" title at the top of your paper. Glue the "Made By" label in the bottom corner, and then write your name on the label.

5 Glue the Sun near one side of the paper. Glue the planets you chose near the Sun.

6 Use a pencil to draw a big oblong oval orbit for the comet. One end of the orbit should be close to the Sun, and the other end should extend across most of the paper. Draw a solid ball for the head of the comet somewhere on your orbit. (Remember, if you want your comet to have a tail, the head must be near the Sun.) If your comet has a tail, use your pencil to draw several lines pointing away from the Sun.

7 Glue the "Sun," "Stars," "Planets," and "Comet" labels next to the corresponding illustrations.

8 Use the chalk to draw an irregular cloud shape. Rub the chalk with your finger to create a white smudged shape for the nebula. Glue the "Nebula" label next to the nebula you created.

9 Place some large and small drops of glue in an arc past the planets. Place your paper in the box top or tray of vermiculite. Sprinkle vermiculite over the glue drops. Tip the paper off into the tray to catch any "asteroids" and "meteors" that did not stick.

10 Glue the "Asteroids & Meteors" label next to these objects.

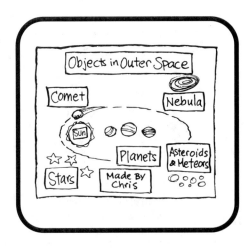

MATERIALS

(per student)

✔ Objects in Outer Space reproducible (page 76)

✔ 12" x 18" (30.5 cm x 46 cm) piece of black construction paper

(per group)

✔ newspaper
✔ old toothbrushes
✔ white tempera paint in a cup
✔ crayons or markers
✔ scissors
✔ glue
✔ chalk
✔ vermiculite
✔ deep box top or tray

Objects in Outer Space

	Made By
Sun	**Planets** **Nebula**
Stars	**Comet** **Asteroids & Meteors**

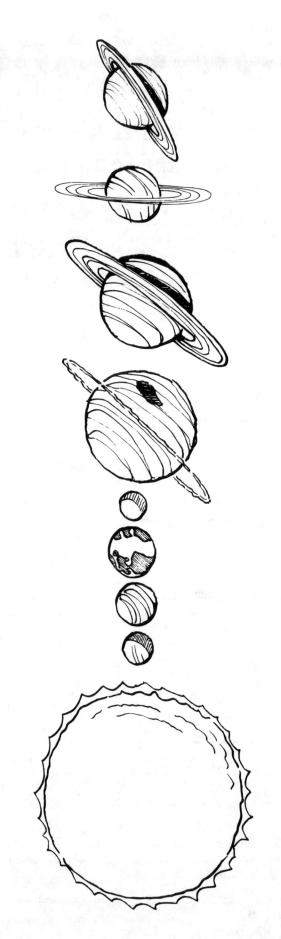

Name _____   Date _____

Wings of a
Butterfly Nebula

Outer Space

What kinds of objects, aside from planets, are found in our solar system and beyond?

Results and Conclusions

1 Why do you think this project was made on black paper?

_____

2 What is the difference between asteroids and meteors?

_____

_____

3 Why do you think you made your nebula with a smudge of chalk?

_____

4 How do nebulae look in space?

_____

5 How is a comet's orbit different from the orbit of a planet?

_____

_____

6 What kinds of objects, aside from planets, are found in our solar system and beyond?

_____

_____

Integrating Science with Reading Instruction · 5–6 © 2002 Creative Teaching Press

Catch a Clue

weathering
and erosion

rocks and minerals

earthquakes

chemical reactions

Our Clues

1 It is in the category of earth science.

2 It is an action that takes place on the surface of the Earth.

3 It occurs all around the world.

4 It occurs slowly.

Integrating Science with Reading Instruction · 5–6 © 2002 Creative Teaching Press

Concept Map

Facts we already know about **weathering and erosion,** and the new facts we have learned

Weathering and Erosion

Word Warm-Up

Which words might you expect to find in a story about **weathering and erosion?**

pressure	Grand Canyon	fragments
changes	exposed	crumble
farmer	cave	evaporates
limestone	chemical	landscape

Integrating Science with Reading Instruction · 5–6 © 2002 Creative Teaching Press

Weathering and Erosion

What is weathering and erosion? Weathering is the breaking down or wearing away of the Earth's surface. It is called erosion when any of the broken-down bits are moved to another location. Wind, water, or ice usually carries these broken-down pieces away. Have you ever seen the Grand Canyon? Is there a delta near you? Maybe you have been to a river or stream. In all of these places, you can see signs of weathering and erosion. Have you ever seen big bulldozers moving soil to prepare the land for a building? Maybe there are floods, landslides, freezing rain, or windstorms where you live. All of these examples cause weathering and erosion.

Weathering happens when rocks are changed forever. The amount of weathering that happens to rocks depends on many factors. These include the structure of the rock, the climate it is in, its location, and how long it is exposed to any conditions that can cause weathering. The weathered material that is left behind could include rock fragments, sand, clay, and soil.

There are two different types of weathering: physical and chemical. Physical weathering occurs when rocks and minerals crumble into smaller pieces. This usually begins at a crack that undergoes pressure or expands. It can also happen because of a change in temperature, water freezing in the cracks, or animals. Imagine a herd of wild horses running over your front yard. This would surely change the landscape! That is what weathering and erosion do to the Earth's surface, but much more slowly. Larger rocks are broken into smaller and smaller rocks. They finally become grains of sand. Did you know that all of the sand at the beach used to be part of bigger rocks?

Chemical weathering occurs when rocks break down due to a chemical reaction and minerals in the rock change. This is what gives some rocks a rusty look. When plants and animals die and decay, acids form that attack the rocks and make them start to crumble. Have you ever visited a

Integrating Science with Reading Instruction · 5–6 © 2002 Creative Teaching Press

cave? Many caves are formed from chemical weathering. The beautiful cave formations are made when water dissolves the limestone in the rock. As the water seeps through the rock, the dissolved limestone moves with it. When the water drips and evaporates, it leaves hardened limestone hanging down from the ceiling or sticking up from the cave floor.

Erosion occurs when water washes away the soil or the wind blows it away. There will be more or less erosion depending on the slope of the land. The steeper or longer the slope of a field, the more chance there is that water will erode the soil.

Erosion occurs naturally as a result of the movements of the wind, water, or ice. Ocean waves pound the shore and wash away the coastline. As glaciers melt and slide down the sides of mountains, they carry away huge quantities of rock and soil. Wind blows sand and soil from one place to another. The sand dunes in a desert are created by the wind.

In most cases, weathering and erosion occur at the same time. Weathering and erosion are similar in the fact that they are both changing the Earth's surface. Since erosion can cause damage, it is important to prevent it whenever we can. What can you do? If you live on a hillside, you can plant trees or other vegetation along the slope. If you cover the soil, it will help reduce erosion because it serves as a "blanket" of protection. You can add mulch such as bark chips, crushed tree leaves, or manure to the soil in your garden. A plant's roots help hold the soil together and prevent erosion. Farmers sometimes plant hillsides to look like shelves to help slow down erosion. The next time you ride in a car or travel on a trip, take a look at the landscape to see if there is any evidence of weathering or erosion.

Integrating Science with Reading Instruction · 5–6 © 2002 Creative Teaching Press

Comprehension Questions

Literal Questions

1. What is the difference between weathering and erosion?

2. What are the different types of weathering? How are they different? What are some examples of each type?

3. Where does weathering or erosion occur? What is the physical evidence that it has occurred?

4. What can be done to prevent further damage due to weathering and erosion?

5. What happens when caves are formed?

Inferential Questions

1. Why is it useful to understand what weathering and erosion are?

2. Why do farmers plant crops year-round if their only concern is to sell strawberries for a few months of the year to make their living?

3. How can you prevent weathering or erosion in your hometown?

4. If you were to visit a desert, do you think you would see any effects from weathering and erosion? Explain what you think you would see.

5. Can you think of an example where weathering and erosion each take place independently of each other? Explain your ideas.

Making Connections

1. Think about a garden or farm that you have seen. What evidence is there that the person who is taking care of the garden or farm is trying to protect the topsoil?

2. Think of different vacation spots that you have either visited or seen images of on television or on posters. What places could you visit to see evidence of weathering and/or erosion?

3. Do you think that you would see any evidence of weathering or erosion if you took a space shuttle and landed on the planet Mars? Why or why not?

4. If you wanted to build a house to live in that would never erode or weather, what would you build the house out of? What would it look like? How long do you predict that it would last? Why is your choice of material superior to bricks?

5. Golfing is a popular sport. What do the owners of golf clubs need to do with regard to weathering and erosion concerns?

Name _____   Date _____

Sharpen Your Skills

1 Physical weathering occurs when rocks and minerals **disintegrate** into smaller pieces.
   What does the word "disintegrate" mean?
   - ○ build up
   - ○ break down
   - ○ dissolve
   - ○ evaporate

2 How would you split the word "weathering" into syllables?
   - ○ wea-ther-ing
   - ○ weath-er-ing
   - ○ we-ather-ing
   - ○ wea-the-ring

3 Which word best completes the following sentence?
   The windowpane is showing some signs of _____.
   - ○ whethering
   - ○ weathering
   - ○ wethering
   - ○ wheathering

4 Erosion occurs **slowly,** so you may not even notice it happening.
   In this sentence, what part of speech is the word "slowly"?
   - ○ adjective
   - ○ adverb
   - ○ preposition
   - ○ conjunction

5 Ocean waves **pound** the shore, washing away the coastline.
   In which of the following sentences is the word "pound" used the same way?
   - ○ Sheila bought a pound of rocks to cover her topsoil.
   - ○ She needed to pound the bricks into the dirt to make her planter.
   - ○ She wondered if she needed to buy another pound of dirt.
   - ○ Later, she found a dog and took it to the pound.

6 Which word would finish this analogy?
   Ocean waves is to **wash away** as **wind** is to _____.
   - ○ blow away
   - ○ melt away
   - ○ evaporate
   - ○ tear away

7 Look at these words: wind–water–clay–ice.
   Which word does not belong with the others?
   - ○ water
   - ○ wind
   - ○ clay
   - ○ ice

Integrating Science with Reading Instruction • 5–6 © 2002 Creative Teaching Press

The Earth Science after-school class at Weaver Elementary is learning about weathering and erosion. Five different speakers are going to teach on five different topics. They brought in some interesting samples for students to touch and slides for them to observe. The speakers are Javier, Anthony, Dawn, Emily, and Emmet. They will be speaking on the following topics: chemical weathering, physical weathering, erosion, preventing erosion, and the Earth's elements. Use the clues below to decide which topic each speaker taught to the class.

Clues

❶ Dawn did not discuss, show samples of, or share slides on weathering.

❷ Emily did not share anything about erosion or the Earth's elements.

❸ Emmet spoke about ideas on how the Earth Science class could make a difference.

❹ The cave slides that Javier showed were amazing!

❺ When it was Anthony's turn to share, he showed the class a picture of a snake coming out of its hole in a vast desert.

	Javier	Anthony	Dawn	Emily	Emmet
Chemical Weathering					
Physical Weathering					
Erosion					
Preventing Erosion					
Earth's Elements					

Javier's topic was _____.

Anthony's topic was _____.

Dawn's topic was _____.

Emily's topic was _____.

Emmet's topic was _____.

Weathering and Erosion

Sand and garden soil mixture

← Pan →

What are some of the ways water changes the Earth's surface?

Teacher Background Information

Although the surface of the Earth appears to be quite hard and resistant, it is always changing. Nothing on the Earth lasts forever. Mountains gradually wear away, the shorelines are altered by the action of ocean waves, the wind blows sand and soil around, and people are forever digging and moving rocks and soil in order to build new streets and homes. The forces of nature slowly but surely break down all rocks. Even the heat of the Sun takes its toll on the structure of rocks. Repeated heating and cooling weakens the rocks, and they begin to crack and crumble. Plant roots force their way in between rocks, causing small cracks to form. Probably the most influential cause of weathering and erosion is the movement of water. This includes water that seeps into rocks and dissolves minerals, water that freezes in cracks or small spaces between rocks, frozen water in the form of glaciers, and the vast quantities of water in the oceans that relentlessly pound the shore. These actions produce both physical and chemical weathering. Chemical weathering is more likely to occur in places where the air is humid or where there is an abundance of water. When carbon dioxide from the air dissolves in water, it forms a weak acid called carbonic acid. This weak acid can dissolve minerals in rocks (especially limestone), making it easier for the remaining rock to crack and crumble. The oxygen in the air can combine with some of the minerals in rocks, which also weakens them. When water washes away the rocks and soil we have erosion. You can buy smooth "river rocks" from a plant nursery or building supply store.

Experiment Results

At the beginning of the experiment, the shale will feel fairly smooth, the sandstone rather gritty, and the limestone hard and perhaps rough. After students shake the container, they most likely will see tiny broken bits of rock. The shale and sandstone are softer and usually break up. The river rocks will have a more rounded shape and a smoother surface texture. This is the result of water flowing over the rocks for a long period of time, wearing away the rough edges. This is an example of physical weathering. The students should observe that they needed to blow a lot of bubbles of carbon dioxide to make their distilled water become acidic. The "acid water" should cause tiny bubbles or slight fizzing from the chalk, which is made of calcium carbonate just like limestone. This indicates it is being slowly dissolved. This happens in nature when limestone caves are formed and is an example of chemical weathering. In the experiment with the soil, the water should wash away a portion of the "hilltop." It may gouge out a narrow section, forming a canyon in their hillside. This is an example of erosion, as the soil is being carried away to another location.

Integrating Science with Reading Instruction · 5–6 © 2002 Creative Teaching Press

Weathering and Erosion

What are some of the ways water changes the Earth's surface?

Integrating Science with Reading Instruction · 5–6 © 2002 Creative Teaching Press

MATERIALS

(per group)

- ✔ samples of sandstone, shale, and limestone
- ✔ plastic container with tight-fitting lid
- ✔ water
- ✔ smooth "river rocks"
- ✔ distilled water
- ✔ plastic cup
- ✔ blue litmus paper
- ✔ straws
- ✔ small piece of chalk
- ✔ rectangular disposable roasting pan, at least 2" (5 cm) deep
- ✔ sand
- ✔ garden soil
- ✔ measuring cup

Procedure

1. Observe the shape and texture of the sandstone, shale, and limestone.

2. Place the samples in the plastic container.

3. Put $\frac{1}{2}$ cup (125 mL) of tap water in the container, and close the lid. Take turns with your group members shaking the container 20–30 times. (This simulates the action of rain on the rocks over many years.)

4. Open the container and observe the rocks. Look for any broken pieces or change in shape or texture.

5. Compare those rocks with the "river rocks." How are they different?

6. Put $\frac{1}{2}$ cup (125 mL) of distilled water into the plastic cup. Insert litmus paper into the cup. (It should stay blue.)

7. Use a straw to gently blow bubbles (carbon dioxide) into the water until the litmus paper turns pink-red. (This indicates the water is now acidic.)

8. Place the chalk in the cup of "bubbled" water. Observe what happens.

9. Fill your roasting pan with a mixture of sand and garden soil. Slope the soil so that you have a tall "hill" on one end of the pan. Moisten the soil with water, and then pack down the soil.

10. Fill the measuring cup with 1 cup (250 mL) of tap water. Hold the cup about 6 inches (15 cm) above the hill, and *slowly* pour all of the water in one spot onto the top of the hill. Observe what happens.

Sand and garden soil mixture

← Pan →

Name _____   Date _____

Weathering and Erosion

What are some of the ways water changes the Earth's surface?

Results and Conclusions

1 Describe how your rocks looked and felt at the beginning of the experiment.

_____

2 Did any of the rocks change after you shook them? _____ If so, how?

_____

3 How are the "river rocks" different from your "rained on" rocks? _____

_____

4 Do the "rained on" rocks illustrate physical weathering, chemical weathering, or erosion?

_____

5 What did the "bubbled" water (acid water) do to the piece of chalk? _____
How or where do you think this might happen in nature?

_____

Does what happened to the piece of chalk illustrate physical weathering, chemical weathering, or erosion?

_____

6 What happened to the soil of your hill when you poured water over the peak?

_____

Does this illustrate physical weathering, chemical weathering, or erosion?

_____

7 What are some of the ways water changes the Earth's surface?

_____

Integrating Science with Reading Instruction · 5–6 © 2002 Creative Teaching Press

Catch a Clue

What will we learn about in our reading today?

climates

ecosystems

energy from the Earth

nutritional choices

Our Clues

1 They are related to the category of earth science.

2 They involve the use of oil, coal, and energy.

3 They are related to conservation.

4 Humans need them to fulfill daily activities.

5 They can be overused.

Integrating Science with Reading Instruction · 5–6 © 2002 Creative Teaching Press

Concept Map

Facts we already know about **energy from the Earth,** and the new facts we have learned

Energy from the Earth

Integrating Science with Reading Instruction · 5–6 © 2002 Creative Teaching Press

Word Warm-Up

Which words might you expect to find in a story about **energy from the Earth?**

elements	resources	reuse
fossil	electricity	polluted
windmills	solar power	reduce
plant	charging	burned

Energy from the Earth

Did you get up this morning and turn on a light? Maybe you took a hot shower. Did you cook any food? Did you ride in a car to school? If you did any of these things, you used energy. What kinds of energy did you use? Where does it all come from?

Let's take a closer look at our energy resources. We can get energy from natural elements like the wind, the Sun, or moving water. We also get energy from fuels. A fuel is anything that gives off heat when it is burned. People used to burn wood for energy to cook food and to make their houses warm.

We also can get energy from fossil fuels. Coal, oil, and natural gas are fossil fuels. They are burned to produce energy—mainly electricity. Coal is created from the remains of plants that lived in swamps thousands of years ago. Today, people dig mines to find the coal. We still have a lot of coal, but our air gets polluted when we burn it. Oil and natural gas come from the remains of many tiny ocean plants and animals. People drill into the ground to find oil and natural gas. Oil is used to produce some electricity. It is also used to produce gasoline for cars, trucks, ships, and planes. Also, oil is used to make many household products. We use natural gas to cook, heat, and produce electricity. Natural gas is the cleanest fossil fuel. It does not cause a lot of air pollution. As you can see, we use a lot of fossil fuels in our daily living!

Resources that provide us with energy are split into two groups: renewable and nonrenewable. Renewable resources are things that we will never run out of. They can replace themselves forever. Renewable resources can also be used to make electricity. Hydropower (falling water), wind energy, solar power, tidal power (wave action caused by the tides), and geothermal (heat from inside the Earth) are all examples of renewable resources.

You have probably seen hydropower and wind energy in action yourself. They have been

Integrating Science with Reading Instruction · 5–6 © 2002 Creative Teaching Press

used for many years. Ships sailed around the world using the wind for power. Have you ever seen an old-fashioned windmill? They were used in many places to produce energy. Today, giant "hi-tech" windmills are used to make electricity.

Solar energy is the cleanest renewable energy. We put solar panels on homes and sometimes on schools to soak up the Sun's energy. This energy is then used to make electricity for lighting, air conditioning, heating water, and charging up solar-powered cars. Do you live in an area with warmer weather throughout the year? If so, you might have solar-powered items all around you! Places with warmer weather can use solar energy better than areas with cooler weather.

Tidal and geothermal energy are not used as much. Tidal power plants must be located along the ocean coast. This is because they use the power of the moving water to make electricity. Geothermal power plants use the heat from inside the Earth to make electricity.

The nonrenewable resources such as coal, oil, and natural gas will be gone someday. This concerns many people because once these resources are gone, we cannot get them back. People are trying to use fewer nonrenewable resources so we do not run out as quickly. What can you do to help? The easiest way for you to help is to practice the "three R's"—reduce, reuse, and recycle. Reduce the amount of waste that you create, reuse materials, and recycle paper, plastic, cans, and bottles. If you practice the three R's, not as many new products will have to be made for you. Then, we will not need to burn as much fossil fuel. If people continue to conserve energy, then our nonrenewable resources will last longer, and we will have a cleaner, healthier environment on Earth.

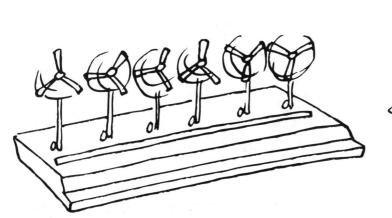

Comprehension Questions

? Literal Questions

1. What are the two main categories of resources? What is the difference between them?
2. What are some examples of renewable resources?
3. What was the earliest fuel used for cooking and heating?
4. What is energy conservation? Why is it related to our Earth's resources?
5. Which fossil fuel is the most abundant today?

? Inferential Questions

1. Why do we need to understand the different types of resources provided by our Earth?
2. Why do you think coal, oil, and natural gas are called fossil fuels?
3. Why do different countries consume different amounts of renewable and nonrenewable resources?
4. Hoover Dam in Nevada is an example of the use of what type of resource? What does it provide? Should more dams be built? Why or why not?
5. Where would solar energy be a good alternative to using fossil fuels? Why would this help the Earth? What areas would not be able to use solar energy as often? Why?

? Making Connections

1. What do you do to conserve energy and save our resources?
2. Why does reducing, reusing, and recycling make a difference? What type of resources are affected?
3. Which alternatives to the use of fossil fuels are possible in your neighborhood or school?
4. Which products around your house do you think are made from oil?
5. If you do not do something today to conserve for tomorrow, what could our Earth look like in 100 years? Be specific and state your reasoning.

Integrating Science with Reading Instruction · 5–6 © 2002 Creative Teaching Press

Name _____ Date _____

Sharpen Your Skills

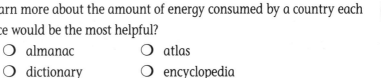

1 If you wanted to learn more about the amount of energy consumed by a country each year, which resource would be the most helpful?

○ almanac   ○ atlas

○ dictionary   ○ encyclopedia

2 **Since** wind that moves over water results in waves, scientists are investigating different uses of wave energy.

In this sentence, what part of speech is the word "since"?

○ adjective   ○ adverb

○ preposition   ○ conjunction

3 Look at these words: solar—wind—tidal—natural gas.

Which word does not belong with the others?

○ solar   ○ wind

○ tidal   ○ natural gas

4 Which words would finish this analogy?

Renewable is to _____ as **nonrenewable** is to _____.

○ coal/solar   ○ natural gas/wind

○ tidal/solar   ○ rain/coal

5 The nonrenewable resources such as coal, oil, and natural gas will be gone someday. This **concerns** many people because once these resources are gone, we cannot get them back.

What does the word "concerns" mean?

○ frustrates   ○ angers

○ worries   ○ saddens

6 If you saw the guide words "record—restraint," which word would <u>not</u> be found on that page of the dictionary?

○ recycle   ○ reduce

○ reuse   ○ resource

7 How many paragraphs were in the story on energy sources?

○ two   ○ four

○ six   ○ eight

Integrating Science with Reading Instruction · 5-6 © 2002 Creative Teaching Press

Name _____   Date _____

Get Logical

Within Serpentine County, there are five major cities: Claymore, Riverdale, Scottsberg, Shrewsberry, and Thomasville. Each of the major cities uses a particular type of resource more than others. The resources the cities use are solar energy, wind energy, wave energy, natural gas, and oil. Use the clues below to decide which type of resource each city uses the most.

Clues

❶ The city of Scottsberg uses too much of a nonrenewable resource. The city has been cited and must develop plans for alternative energy consumption.

❷ The cities of Claymore and Shrewsberry do not use any form of wave energy.

❸ Neither the city of Scottsberg nor Shrewsberry relies upon the use of oil.

❹ A survey of the households in the city of Shrewsberry found that 85% of the homes were heated by the Sun.

❺ The city of Riverdale uses many windmills to produce energy.

	Claymore	Riverdale	Scottsberg	Shrewsberry	Thomasville
Solar Energy					
Wind Energy					
Wave Energy					
Natural Gas					
Oil					

Claymore uses _____.

Riverdale uses _____.

Scottsberg uses _____.

Shrewsberry uses _____.

Thomasville uses _____.

Integrating Science with Reading Instruction · 5–6 © 2002 Creative Teaching Press

Energy from the Earth

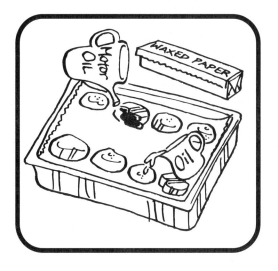

Why do we have to drill into the ground to find deposits of oil and natural gas?

Teacher Background Information

From early times, wood was the most important resource that provided us with energy because it was easy to obtain and use. Coal became the next energy source to become popular. Half a ton of coal can produce as much energy as burning 2 tons of wood. It also costs a lot less. Coal became the fuel for trains, steamboats, factories, and home heating. With the advent of the automobile, oil became an important energy source. Since oil and natural gas are often found together, natural gas use also increased. Today, we are dependent upon oil and natural gas for most of our energy needs. Most surface coal has been extracted, and we must dig mines to find other coal deposits. Oil and natural gas form mainly under the ocean or in places that used to be under an ocean many years ago. Layers of dead plant and animal plankton are the main ingredients in this resource. Oil is lighter than water, so it tends to seep up towards the surface through the rock layers. This is how it was first discovered. Today, all the surface pools of oil are gone, and we have to drill down into the Earth to find trapped pools of oil and natural gas. You can save the rocks after the experiment, wash them in detergent, and use them again another time, if you wish. For the household oil used in the experiment, you can buy "3 in 1 oil" from a hardware store.

Experiment Results

The oil will not mix with the water. After a few minutes, the students should see a thin layer of oil on top of the water. This happens because oil is less dense than water. Some of the oil should be absorbed into some of the rocks. The sandstone absorbs the oil better and faster. The household oil will be absorbed better than the motor oil. Motor oil is thicker (more viscous) and is absorbed much more slowly. The shale rock is the hardest for the oil to penetrate. Therefore, pools of oil get trapped beneath layers of shale. If oil and natural gas are found together, natural gas will be at the top of the underground pocket. Natural gas (methane) is much lighter and will rise up as far as possible. Today, we have to drill into the ground to find deposits of oil and natural gas because we have used up our surface deposits and the remaining deposits are trapped under impermeable rock layers.

Integrating Science with Reading Instruction · 5–6 © 2002 Creative Teaching Press

Energy from the Earth

Why do we have to drill into the ground to find deposits of oil and natural gas?

Procedure

1 Fill the measuring cup about half full of water.

2 Add a large squirt of household oil to the water, and observe for a few minutes.

3 Line the tray with waxed paper.

4 Place all the pieces of sandstone, limestone, and shale in two identical rows in the tray.

5 Pour one drop of household oil on <u>one</u> piece of <u>each</u> kind of rock in the first row.

6 Place one drop of motor oil on the other piece of each kind of rock in the second row.

7 Wait 5 minutes. Observe each rock on the top, the side, and the bottom. Look to see if the oil is still sitting on top of the rock or if it was absorbed by the rock.

MATERIALS

(per group)
- ✔ measuring cup
- ✔ water
- ✔ small can of household oil
- ✔ small tray
- ✔ waxed paper
- ✔ 2 pieces each of sandstone, limestone, and shale
- ✔ dropper bottle of motor oil

Integrating Science with Reading Instruction · 5–6 © 2002 Creative Teaching Press

Name _____   Date _____

Energy from the Earth

Why do we have to drill into the ground to find deposits of oil and natural gas?

Results and Conclusions

❶ What happened when you added the oil to the water?

_____

❷ How did it look after a few minutes? _____
Why do you think this happened?

_____

❸ Was any oil absorbed by any of the rocks?_____ If so, which ones?

_____

❹ Which rock seemed to absorb the oil better or faster?

_____

❺ Which type of oil was absorbed better or faster?

_____

❻ Which type of rock was the hardest for the oil to get through?

_____

❼ Under which kind of rock would you expect to find oil collecting?

_____

❽ If you were to drill into the ground and find oil and natural gas together, which one would you expect
to find first? _____Why?

_____

❾ Why do we have to drill into the ground to find deposits of oil and natural gas?

_____

Integrating Science with Reading Instruction · 5–6 © 2002 Creative Teaching Press

Catch a Clue

What will we learn about in our reading today?

wedge

medicine

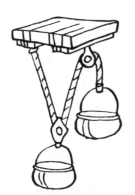

pulley

oil production

Our Clues

1 It is used by people all over the world.

2 It enhances our life.

3 It has different parts.

4 You can make it yourself.

5 It is a simple machine.

Integrating Science with Reading Instruction · 5–6 © 2002 Creative Teaching Press

Concept Map

Facts we already know about **pulleys,** and the new facts we have learned

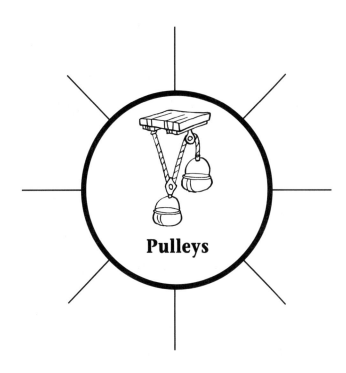

Pulleys

Word Warm-Up

Which words might you expect to find in a story about **pulleys?**

weight	groove	effort
attached	changing	distance
flagpole	direction	skateboard
library	moveable	convenient

Integrating Science with Reading Instruction · 5–6 © 2002 Creative Teaching Press

Pulleys

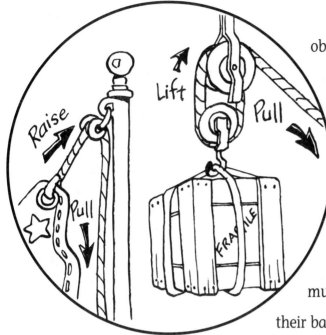

Do you ever work hard trying to lift a heavy object? Does it make you tired? A pulley could help make your work easier. A pulley is a type of simple machine. It uses a wheel with a groove in the rim and a rope, belt, or chain wrapped around the wheel. The groove keeps the rope from slipping off of the pulley.

People all over the world use pulleys in many different ways to help make their work much easier. Farmers use them to raise hay bales into their barns, construction workers use them to move loads of materials, and rock climbers use them to safely climb rocks. Pulleys are useful for moving heavy objects and to move things sideways. Pulleys are used on exercise equipment, flagpoles, cranes, curtain rods, and in cars.

There are two kinds of pulleys to help you with different kinds of work. One is called a fixed pulley. The fixed pulley does not move from one place to another. It is "fixed" or attached in place. It helps by changing the direction of your work. For example, if you want to raise the flag at your school, a fixed pulley can make it much easier. Without a pulley, you would have to climb up the flagpole with the flag, attach it, and then climb down. At the end of the day, you would have to do this again to unhook the flag and bring it down. That is a lot of work just to get the flag up the flagpole! This can be made much easier with the help of a fixed pulley at the top of the flagpole. A long loop of rope runs around the pulley wheel. As someone pulls down on the rope, the flag moves up. The fixed pulley changed the direction of your pulling. It was easier to pull down to make the flag move up. When it is time to lower the flag, all you need to do is pull down on the other side of the rope. Fixed pulleys do not give you any added force or strength while doing the work. They are mainly used in changing the direction of your work. It is not impossible to raise a flag without the help of a fixed pulley. It is just more convenient to do it with a pulley.

Integrating Science with Reading Instruction · 5–6 © 2002 Creative Teaching Press

The other kind of pulley is a moveable pulley. A moveable pulley is attached to the object that you are moving. It moves along the rope with whatever is being moved. Moveable pulleys do not change the direction of your work, but they do make the work easier for you. It takes less effort to do the work when you use a moveable pulley, but you have to pull over a larger distance. Imagine you wanted to lift a bucket full of heavy bricks to the roof of a building. If you stood on the top of the roof and just used your muscles to lift the bucket of bricks, you would have to pull up the full weight of the bricks. You could attach the bucket of bricks to a moveable pulley by running a long rope from the roof, around the pulley wheel, and back up to your hands. Then, you could pull up on the rope to raise the bricks with much less effort. The pulley would help you do your work. Moveable pulleys lessen the force or effort you need to do work.

You can combine fixed and moveable pulleys, too. This lets you change the direction of your work and makes the work easier to do. Each fixed pulley changes the direction of your effort, and each moveable pulley lowers the amount of force or effort needed. The more moveable pulleys you use, the easier the work becomes. An example of a combined pulley is called a block and tackle. The "block" is a group of pulleys connected by a frame and some hooks. The "tackle" is how the blocks and ropes are arranged to lift the objects. You can see a block and tackle on weight machines in gyms and when you see people wash the windows of high-rise buildings. How would movers get a piano onto the tenth floor of a building without an elevator? They would use a block and tackle pulley system. The use of many pulleys lets you lift very heavy objects with much less effort.

As you can tell, if you need to lift anything heavy, then a pulley is a simple machine that could make your work easier. People all over the world use pulleys in their jobs and homes. Look around you. What kinds of pulleys do you use? When would a pulley make the work you do easier?

Integrating Science with Reading Instruction · 5–6 © 2002 Creative Teaching Press

Comprehension Questions

? Literal Questions

❶ What is a pulley? What does it do? Why is it useful?

❷ What are the different types of pulleys? How are they similar and how are they different?

❸ What kind of a pulley is a flagpole?

❹ Who uses pulleys and how do they use pulleys for their jobs?

❺ How does a fixed pulley change the way you do your work? A moveable pulley?

? Inferential Questions

❶ How does a pulley help people do work all around the world?

❷ Mr. McGinnis lives on the third floor of an apartment building. He is moving to the sixth floor. He has a huge rock waterfall that sits on his extra large balcony. How can he get his waterfall to the sixth floor when it will not even fit through the door? Explain your answer in detail.

❸ Carl has a tree house. He has to climb the tree using both hands to get up to his tree house because it is 15 feet (4.58 m) above the ground, and he is not allowed to climb on the ladder. (He fell once and broke his arm!) He wants to get his handheld video game, three heavy books, and a bottle of water up to the tree house. He does not have a backpack. How could you help Carl?

❹ Why was the invention of the pulley important to all people?

❺ Who do you think uses pulleys the most—people in third world countries or in more civilized areas?

? Making Connections

❶ Think of three occupations. Would a pulley help the worker of each occupation? Why or why not?

❷ How are pulleys used to make work easier at school? At home? On a farm?

❸ How do you think pulleys were invented? Why do you think they were invented?

❹ If you had to put a pulley in your bedroom, where would you put it and what would you use it for?

❺ Which pulley would you be interested in making and why? What materials would you need?

Integrating Science with Reading Instruction · 5-6 © 2002 Creative Teaching Press

Sharpen Your Skills

1 Moveable pulleys allow you to **exert** less force to move objects.

Which word is a synonym for the word "exert"?

- ○ use
- ○ take up
- ○ save
- ○ waste

2 If you wanted to learn more about different types of pulleys and other machines that make work easier, which person should you talk to?

- ○ veterinarian
- ○ teacher
- ○ construction worker
- ○ secretary

3 As long as you get more out **of** it than you have to put into it, then you will have a mechanical advantage.

In this sentence, what part of speech is the word "of"?

- ○ adjective
- ○ preposition
- ○ adverb
- ○ conjunction

4 You can open and close venetian blinds with one easy pull on the cord, instead of **manually adjusting** each piece individually.

What do the words "manually adjusting" mean?

- ○ fixing them to match
- ○ adjusting them with a pulley
- ○ moving them with your hands
- ○ changing them with a manual

5 Which words would finish this analogy?

Fixed pulley is to _____ as **moveable pulley** is to _____.

- ○ bucket/wagon
- ○ flag/bucket
- ○ flag/wagon
- ○ flag/block and tackle

6 Look at these words: moveable—changeable—understandable.

What do you think the suffix "able" means?

- ○ in the act of
- ○ beginning to
- ○ looking for
- ○ capable of

7 If you saw the imaginary formula P = LW, and it was related to what you read in the story, what would it best represent?

- ○ pulley = lots of work
- ○ pulley = less work
- ○ pulley = lucky worker
- ○ pulley = little workers

Integrating Science with Reading Instruction · 5–6 © 2002 Creative Teaching Press

Get Logical

It does not matter what career you choose to do when you get older, a simple machine will surely make it much easier. Bobby, Darren, Flo, Heather, and Jared are all hard workers, but they realize that simple machines could make their work a little bit easier. They each use a specific tool at work. The tools they use include a fixed pulley, a moveable pulley, a combined pulley, a wedge, and a wheel. Use the clues below to decide which tool each person uses.

Clues

❶ Flo does not use a tool that involves a wheel.

❷ Bobby uses his tool to help him wash the windows on a high-rise building.

❸ Heather, the principal, conducts a flag ceremony every Friday morning that includes the entire school.

❹ Jared lifted a bucket of bricks to the second floor of a building with this tool.

	Bobby	Darren	Flo	Heather	Jared
Fixed Pulley					
Moveable Pulley					
Combined Pulley					
Wedge					
Wheel					

Bobby uses a _____.

Darren uses a _____.

Flo uses a _____.

Heather uses a _____.

Jared uses a _____.

Integrating Science with Reading Instruction · 5–6 © 2002 Creative Teaching Press

Pulleys

How do fixed and moveable pulleys help us do our work?

Teacher Background Information

Fixed pulleys can change the direction of your work, but they cannot add any force to your effort. To lift 50 pounds (22.7 kg) of bricks with a fixed pulley takes 50 pounds of muscle effort. Use a moveable pulley when you have a load that is too heavy to lift or move with just your own effort. Moveable pulleys create what is called "mechanical advantage." When we apply a small force on a machine and the machine gives us more force or lifts or moves a heavy object, then we achieve an advantage over doing the work without the machine. As long as we get more effort out of the machine than we put in, we have achieved a mechanical advantage. If a machine has a mechanical advantage of four, that means it is four times easier to do the work with the machine than without it. Block and tackle pulley systems use multiple moveable pulleys, increasing the mechanical advantage even more. A block and tackle system will often allow someone to lift an extremely heavy object with minimal effort. Pulleys are available at hardware stores as well as through science supply catalogs. They come with small hooks so that you can attach them in place and/or add a hanging bucket with weights. As an option, you could use a spring scale to actually measure the amount of effort needed for each experiment. Or, students can just tell the difference by the way it feels (harder or easier to lift).

Experiment Results

In step 5, students are testing a fixed pulley. It is not any easier to lift the bucket this way than in step 3 when they just use their muscles. All the fixed pulley does is change the direction of the way the work was done (pulling down instead of up). In steps 6 and 7, students test a moveable pulley. It will be easier to lift the bucket with the moveable pulley, as the pulley is doing part of the work. (It is actually twice as easy.) The block and tackle is a combination of both fixed and moveable pulleys. It will be much easier for students to lift the bucket this way, as they have several moveable pulleys that give added mechanical advantage. The fixed pulleys are at the top of the block and tackle, and the moveable pulleys are at the bottom. In everyday life, we use fixed pulleys on flagpoles, on drapes, and in car engines (fan belt wheels). Single moveable pulleys are used on some exercise equipment or for lifting hay into a barn. Block and tackle systems are used in construction cranes, by people who wash windows on the side of skyscrapers, and by car mechanics when they need to lift out a car's engine.

Integrating Science with Reading Instruction · 5–6 © 2002 Creative Teaching Press

Pulleys

How do fixed and moveable pulleys help us do our work?

Procedure

1 Place the chart stand on a table. Cut a small piece of string. Tie and knot it into a loop around the top of the chart stand.

2 Hang the single pulley from the loop.

3 Fill the bucket with the weights. Lift the bucket with one arm using only your muscle power. Notice how heavy it feels.

4 Cut a long piece of string. Tie it to the bucket handle, and loop it over the pulley wheel and down towards the table. (You can tape the free end of the string to the bottom of the chart stand to keep it from falling off.)

5 Pull down on the string to lift the bucket. Notice how much muscle effort was needed.

6 Attach the single pulley to the bucket handle (using the hook or tie with the string). Cut a long piece of string. Tie one end to the top of the chart stand, and then loop it under the pulley wheel and back up to the top of the chart stand. (You can tape the free end to the top of the chart stand to keep it from falling off.)

7 Pull up on the string to lift the bucket. Notice how much muscle effort was needed.

8 Set up your block and tackle pulley system. (You can tape the free end of the string to the bottom of the chart stand to keep it from falling off.)

9 Pull down on the string to lift the bucket. Notice how much muscle effort was needed.

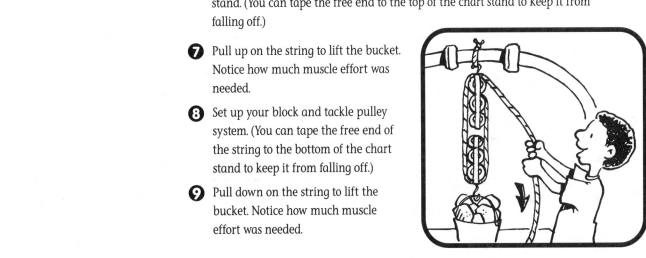

Integrating Science with Reading Instruction • 5–6 © 2002 Creative Teaching Press

MATERIALS

(per group)
- ✔ small chart stand
- ✔ scissors
- ✔ string
- ✔ single pulley
- ✔ small bucket with a handle
- ✔ 2 lb. (1 kg) weights (e.g, fishing weights or rocks)
- ✔ masking tape (optional)
- ✔ block and tackle (2 triple pulley sets)

Pulleys

How do fixed and moveable pulleys help us do our work?

Results and Conclusions

❶ In step 5, were you testing a fixed or moveable pulley?

_____

Was it easier to lift the bucket with the pulley or without it? _____

Why or why not?

_____

❷ In step 6, were you testing a fixed or moveable pulley? _____

Was it any easier to lift the bucket with the pulley arranged this way? _____
Why or why not?

_____

❸ When you set up your block and tackle, what kind(s) of pulleys were you using—fixed, moveable, or both?

_____

Was it any easier to lift the bucket with the pulleys arranged this way?

_____

Why or why not?

_____

❹ Can you think of an example in everyday life where a fixed, single moveable, or a block and tackle pulley would be useful?

❺ How do fixed and moveable pulleys help us do our work?

_____

Integrating Science with Reading Instruction · 5–6 © 2002 Creative Teaching Press

Catch a Clue

What will we learn about in our reading today?

solutions

medicines

heat energy

sound energy

Our Clues

1 It is something that is important for our survival.

2 It can be moved from one place to another.

3 It involves molecules.

4 It is related to how fast the molecules move.

5 We can record its temperature.

Concept Map

Facts we already know about **heat energy,** and the new facts we have learned

Heat Energy

Integrating Science with Reading Instruction · 5–6 © 2002 Creative Teaching Press

Word Warm-Up

Which words might you expect to find in a story about **heat energy?**

particles	conductor	radiation
molecules	transferred	expand
ice cube	currents	movement
balance	chocolate	solar

Heat Energy

Rub your hands together very quickly. Are they beginning to feel hot? You just created heat energy! The more you rubbed your hands against each other, the more heat energy you created. When you think of energy, you probably think of whether or not you are tired or full of energy. Energy is what makes things happen. It makes grass grow, cars move, computers work, and stars explode.

All materials are made of tiny particles called molecules. These molecules are always moving. The movement of these molecules creates heat. The amount of heat created depends on how fast the molecules move. The faster they move, the hotter it will get. Usually, as molecules move faster, they take up more space and make objects expand.

Heat can be transferred from one object to another. It can be transferred in three different ways: conduction, convection, or radiation. The type of material something is made of makes a difference in how heat is transferred. You see this when a cup of hot chocolate cools off. Your cup gets warmer and your hot chocolate gets cooler. This is called conduction. Solids transfer heat through conduction. Imagine that you and four friends are standing next to each other in a line, with your elbows touching. The first person bumps the person next to him. Then, that person bumps the person next in line, and so on. You have "conducted" this movement down the line. This is how heat would travel if you and your friends were molecules in a metal bar. Molecules bump into other molecules, which makes them move faster. An object gets hotter from the movement of the molecules. The heat energy has been passed, or conducted, from molecule to molecule within the metal bar. The metal bar itself did not move. It just got hotter. All solid objects conduct heat, although some are better conductors than others. Good heat conductors are usually made out of metal. Some pots and pans have metal handles that become hot. That is why hot pads are so popular! Other pots and pans have

Integrating Science with Reading Instruction · 5-6 © 2002 Creative Teaching Press

handles made out of poor conductors like wood or plastic. They keep the heat from traveling through the handle and to your hand.

Liquids and gases transfer heat better through convection. Convection is when heat makes the molecules in an object spread out. Convection occurs when hot air rises above cooler air. The movement of the air molecules creates air currents. Warm air rises and cooler air sinks. These convection currents also occur in water. Have you ever been swimming in a lake or in the ocean and felt the water at your feet was colder than the water near your shoulders? This is because of convection.

Radiation is a means of heat travel that is very different from conduction and convection. Radiation is the release of invisible heat rays from a fire or from the sun. It does not rely on moving molecules to transfer heat. Heat waves can travel, or radiate, through outer space where there are no air molecules. For example, when the radiant energy from the sun hits a solid object like the earth, the earth soaks up the energy and changes it into heat. This is how the sun heats the earth even though the sun is 93 million miles (150 million km) away.

Whenever a hot object is placed near a cold object, the hot object will transfer heat to the cold object until they reach a state of balance. A balance happens when their temperatures are the same. The fast moving molecules mix with the slow moving molecules until they are all mixed and balanced. Imagine putting an ice cube into a cup of hot chocolate. The hot chocolate has molecules that are moving around very quickly. The heat energy from the hot chocolate will transfer to the ice cube. That will make the ice cube melt. Then, your hot chocolate will not be hot anymore. The water in the ice and the hot chocolate achieved a state of heat balance.

Heat energy is a form of energy that usually involves molecules in motion. It can be changed or transferred through conduction, convection, or radiation. Everything on earth relies on heat energy.

Comprehension Questions

Literal Questions

1. What are the three different ways that heat can be transferred from one object to another? Explain each method.

2. What types of materials are good conductors of heat?

3. What types of materials are poor conductors of heat?

4. Which method of transferring heat does not rely on the movement of molecules? Explain.

5. Where is the coldest part of the ocean?

Inferential Questions

1. How fast do you think the molecules are moving in the refrigerator as compared to the freezer? Explain your thinking.

2. How do you think solar panels work? How can heat energy be used?

3. What is the best material for making solar panels?

4. If it were a very cold day, which would keep you warmer—a leather jacket or a wool jacket? Why?

5. Some people have convection ovens. What do you think these ovens do? How would you expect them to be different from regular ovens?

Making Connections

1. Describe three different ways in which you can generate some heat energy. Try them. Which method generated the most heat?

2. When the weather reporter on the news tells you the temperature for the day, what is he measuring it with? What is today's approximate temperature? Are the molecules moving faster or slower as compared to yesterday? Explain your thinking.

3. When you go to a Mexican restaurant and order fajitas, why do you think they are cooked in a metal pan and then served in the metal pan on a wood tray? Explain.

4. Have you ever gone down a slide on a hot summer day in a pair of shorts? How did that feel? Why do you think it felt that way?

5. Have you ever seen pictures of hot air balloons in magazines or on television? How do they work?

Integrating Science with Reading Instruction · 5–6 © 2002 Creative Teaching Press

Sharpen Your Skills

1 Which words best complete the following sentence?

Solids transfer heat best through _____, while liquids and gases transfer heat best through _____.

○ radiation/conduction   ○ conduction/radiation
○ convection/conduction   ○ conduction/convection

2 If you wanted to check whether or not the word "conduction" had multiple meanings, which resource would be the most helpful?

○ dictionary   ○ atlas
○ Internet   ○ almanac

3 When pet rabbits are hot and kept in a cage, it is suggested that the owner put a frozen bottle of water in the cage next to the rabbits. Which method of heat transfer would then occur to "cool down" the rabbits?

○ conduction   ○ convection
○ radiation   ○ transfer

4 All solid objects conduct heat, **although** some are better conductors than others.

In this sentence, what part of speech is the word "although"?

○ adjective   ○ adverb
○ preposition   ○ conjunction

5 Look at these words: heat—ruler—temperature—thermometer.

Which word does not belong with the others?

○ heat   ○ ruler
○ temperature   ○ thermometer

6 Which words would finish this analogy?

Fast molecules are to _____ as **slow molecules** are to _____.

○ hot/cold   ○ cold/hot
○ hot/hot   ○ cold/cold

7 Dr. Miles is an expert on radiation therapy.

"Dr." is a(n) _____ for the word "doctor."

○ acronym   ○ analogy
○ pseudonym   ○ abbreviation

Integrating Science with Reading Instruction · 5-6 © 2002 Creative Teaching Press

Get Logical

Name _____   Date _____

The students at Colby Cooking School are learning about heat energy so they can better understand what is happening to their food when they cook. Every student enrolled in the school wants to become a chef and work in a fine dining restaurant. The chefs-in-training include Margo, Hector, Tasha, Kurran, and Sydney. Each trainee is responsible for learning about one of the following aspects of heat energy: conduction, convection, radiation, temperature, and methods of increasing heat energy. Use the clues below to decide which aspect of heat energy each chef-in-training learned about.

Clues

❶ Kurran and Hector did not learn about one of the methods of transferring heat.

❷ The chef-in-training who focused on reading thermometers was not Hector or Margo.

❸ Either Hector or Tasha investigated the release of invisible heat rays.

❹ Margo learned about transferring heat through liquids and gases, not solids.

	Margo	Hector	Tasha	Kurran	Sydney
Conduction					
Convection					
Radiation					
Temperature					
Increasing Heat Energy					

Margo learned about _____.

Hector learned about _____.

Tasha learned about _____.

Kurran learned about _____.

Sydney learned about _____.

Integrating Science with Reading Instruction · 5–6 © 2002 Creative Teaching Press

Heat Energy

How are the three ways that heat travels different from each other?

Teacher Background Information

We commonly use thermometers to measure the temperature of the air, water, or even our own bodies (if we think we might be sick). The temperatures measured in this experiment will give an indication of the relative amount of heat energy. When you use thermometers with students, be sure they know the correct way to hold them and read them. The bulb at the bottom of the thermometer is what is taking the reading. Advise students not to hold the thermometer at the bottom. Otherwise, they will be taking the temperature of their thumb or finger. Most common thermometers are filled with either a red alcohol solution or mercury. Mercury thermometers will have a silver liquid in the bulb and tube. Almost all thermometers are made of glass, so caution students to handle them carefully. Alcohol thermometers are recommended for student use, since mercury is poisonous and is difficult to clean up if a thermometer is dropped and broken. Most thermometer scales are divided so that each line represents one or two degrees of temperature. A radiometer is a device made of four little vanes, painted black on one side and white on the other. The vanes are balanced upon a pin so that they can turn freely. The black vanes absorb light and turn it into heat. The white vanes reflect more of the light. The entire apparatus is encased inside a glass ball, which has had the air removed. A radiometer shows how heat can travel through outer space, where there is no air to create convection currents. The hotter black vanes will cause the apparatus to spin. A radiometer can be purchased from a hobby shop or science supply store.

Experiment Results

The vanes of the radiometer will spin after being exposed to the flashlight. The black vanes absorb light and turn it into heat. The white vanes reflect more of the light. As the light strikes the black vanes, they become hotter and begin to move. As more heat is absorbed, the vanes spin faster. The heat travels to the vanes by radiation. There is no air inside the glass ball for convection currents to form. When the nail is held over the flame, the wax bump on the other end will begin to melt. The heat travels through the nail by conduction. The students should notice that when red food coloring is added to cold and hot water there is a difference in the way the food coloring mixes. The molecules of hot water are moving more rapidly, causing the red food coloring to mix more rapidly in the hot water than in the cold water. It is important that the students do not shake, stir, or disturb the two glasses. This way they can observe the movement of the convection currents in the water. The food coloring is colder than the hot water, and this will cause convection currents to mix the two more quickly. Heat travels by conduction through solids, by convection through liquids and gases, and by radiation through outer space or anywhere it does not use molecules to travel.

Heat Energy

How are the three ways that heat travels different from each other?

Procedure

1 Shine the flashlight (sun) on the radiometer. Observe what happens to the little vanes. (Remember, there is no air inside the glass.)

2 Place a piece of waxed paper on your desk. Have your teacher use a match to light your candle. Set the nail on the waxed paper on your desk, and carefully drip melted wax near the pointed end of the nail to make a bump of wax. Blow out the candle.

3 Have your teacher light your alcohol lamp. Put the clothespin near the head of the nail.

4 Hold the clothespin and heat the <u>middle</u> of the nail over the alcohol lamp for a few minutes. Observe the candle wax at the end of the nail. Extinguish the flame of the alcohol lamp.

5 Fill one glass with hot water. Fill the other glass with cold water.

6 Put a thermometer in each glass. Read each temperature, and record your findings on your Results and Conclusions reproducible, question #7.

7 Add two drops of food coloring to each glass, and observe what happens.

MATERIALS

(per group)
- ✔ flashlight
- ✔ radiometer
- ✔ waxed paper
- ✔ matches (teacher use only)
- ✔ candle
- ✔ 4" (10 cm) nail
- ✔ alcohol lamp
- ✔ clothespin
- ✔ 2 glasses
- ✔ water
- ✔ 2 thermometers
- ✔ red food coloring

Integrating Science with Reading Instruction · 5–6 © 2002 Creative Teaching Press

Name _____ Date _____

Heat Energy

How are the three ways that heat travels different from each other?

Results and Conclusions

1 What happened to the little vanes of the radiometer?

_____

2 Why do you think some of the vanes are black and others are white?

_____

3 What caused the changes you observed on the radiometer?

_____

4 How did heat travel to the little vanes?

_____

5 What happened when you held the center of the nail over the flame? _____

Why do you think this happened?

_____

6 How did the heat travel down the nail?

_____

7 What was the temperature of the cold water? _____ The hot water? _____

8 What happened when you put red food coloring in the cold water?

_____

What happened when you put red food coloring in the hot water?

_____

Was there any difference? _____ If so, why?

_____

9 How are the three ways that heat travels different from each other?

_____

Integrating Science with Reading Instruction · 5–6 © 2002 Creative Teaching Press

Catch a Clue

What will we learn about in our reading today?

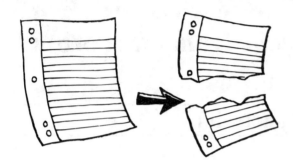

physical and
chemical changes

atoms
and molecules

scientific
laboratories

currents and rivers

Our Clues

1 They are in the area of scientific research called physical science.

2 They are especially important for pharmacists and chemists to understand.

3 They can take place anywhere.

4 You make them every day.

5 They can be temporary or permanent.

Integrating Science with Reading Instruction · 5–6 © 2002 Creative Teaching Press

Concept Map

Facts we already know about **physical and chemical changes,** and the new facts we have learned

Physical and Chemical Changes

Integrating Science with Reading Instruction · 5–6 © 2002 Creative Teaching Press

Word Warm-Up

Which words might you expect to find in a story about **physical and chemical changes?**

matter	state	reaction
reversible	carbon	rubber band
evaporates	molecules	dissolves
ingredients	solution	lightning

Integrating Science with Reading Instruction · 5–6 © 2002 Creative Teaching Press

Physical and Chemical Changes

Get a piece of paper. How can you change it? You can crumple it up into a ball. You can fold it into small squares. You can tear it in half. Whatever you did to make this piece of paper different, you created a physical change in matter.

Matter can be changed. Matter can go through two different kinds of changes. They are physical and chemical. A physical change is reversible, but a chemical change is not. Physical changes involve a change in the form, size, or shape of the matter, but you still have the original material. For example, if you tore your paper in half, you still had paper. When matter is changed chemically, it cannot return to its original state. If you were to burn the paper, then you would no longer have any paper at all. The chemical change has forever changed your paper. It is now a pile of black ash called carbon. The carbon is a new material that was formed as a result of the chemical change. This tells you that a chemical reaction has taken place. When you change matter, ask yourself two questions: Does the material still look the same? If not, can you change it back? If it looks different and you cannot change it back, then you know that you observed a chemical reaction that resulted in a chemical change.

You make physical changes to matter every day. When you stretch a rubber band, you change its shape by expanding the ends. It is reversible, since you can let go of the rubber band and it will be in its original shape once again. Physical changes also include changing the state of matter. This is a change in its form. When a solid melts or a liquid freezes or evaporates, a physical change has happened. When one substance dissolves into another substance, it is a bit harder to tell what type of physical change occurred. For example, if you put a sugar cube in a glass of water, the molecules of the sugar will separate and spread out. When one substance dissolves in another, a solution is created. You cannot see the pieces of the solid that dissolved in the water, but they are

Integrating Science with Reading Instruction · 5–6 © 2002 Creative Teaching Press

still there. If you taste the water, you would discover the sugar is still present. When a solution is made, the molecules of the solid separate and mix in between the water molecules. There will be sugar molecules at the top of the water, in the middle of the glass, and at the bottom of the glass. They will keep mixing until they are evenly distributed throughout the water. Can you think of how you could separate the sugar molecules from the water molecules? You should be able to get back your original ingredients if it is a physical change.

You make chemical changes in matter every day, too. Cooking dinner and eating it are both examples of chemical changes. After you have cooked the food, it looks different and tastes different. You cannot make it go back to the way it was before. It has been changed permanently. For example, scrambled eggs cannot return to being an egg in a shell. In order to have a chemical change, energy is either required or released during the chemical reaction. If energy is released, it is usually given off in the form of heat. If energy is required, you may have to add heat to make the reaction take place.

There are different types of chemical reactions that can take place. They are combination, decomposition, and replacement reactions. A combination reaction is when atoms and/or molecules combine to form a new type of matter. A decomposition reaction is when the original matter decomposes, or splits up, into two or more compounds and/or elements. A replacement reaction can be a single or double replacement reaction. In a single replacement reaction, one substance replaces another. In a double replacement reaction, two substances change places to form new compounds.

As you can see, all matter can be changed either physically or chemically. The important thing to remember is the result of each type of action. Once you perform a chemical reaction, your original piece of matter cannot be retrieved. However, if you make a physical change in the matter, the original matter remains the same. It has just changed form, shape, or appearance. Physical and chemical changes occur all around us every day. Look around. What types of changes do you see happening to matter in your environment?

Integrating Science with Reading Instruction · 5–6 © 2002 Creative Teaching Press

Comprehension Questions

Literal Questions

1. What are the two different ways that matter can be changed? Which is temporary and which is permanent?
2. Which reactions are opposites?
3. What is decomposition? What kind of a change to matter is it?
4. What are the different types of chemical reactions that can happen?
5. Give three examples of physical changes to matter that you can do in your classroom.

Inferential Questions

1. What is happening when you make hot chocolate by mixing the cocoa powder with the water and heating it up?
2. Which type of changes do you think you make the most? Why?
3. Which types of changes to matter do you think are the most dangerous? Why?
4. Why is it important to understand the different ways to change matter? How does changing matter relate to you?
5. Why do you think people used to burn their trash instead of throwing it away?

Making Connections

1. Imagine that you are outside for snack and recess. Describe two physical changes and two chemical changes that you can make while you are out at recess.
2. Which type of chemical reaction takes place when hydrogen peroxide is heated and separates into hydrogen and oxygen?
3. When making chemical reactions, it would be wise to take what types of safety precautions? Why?
4. How is matter being changed on the Fourth of July every year all across America?
5. Jonah's baby sister would not take her medicine, so his dad mixed it in with her juice and put it in her bottle. Jonah's sister drank the juice and the medicine. What happened in terms of physical and chemical changes?

Integrating Science with Reading Instruction · 5–6 © 2002 Creative Teaching Press

Name _____   Date _____

Sharpen Your Skills

1 In a chemical reaction, the original state of matter has been **permanently** changed.
Which word is an antonym for the word "permanently"?
- ○ forever
- ○ always
- ○ temporarily
- ○ partially

2 If you wanted to learn more about making chemical reactions, which of the following people would be the most helpful?
- ○ carpenter
- ○ pharmacist
- ○ psychologist
- ○ veterinarian

3 How would you split the word "combination" into syllables?
- ○ com-binati-on
- ○ com-bi-na-tion
- ○ co-mbin-ation
- ○ com-bin-a-tion

4 In the word "chemist," "-ist" is known as the _____.
- ○ prefix
- ○ adjective
- ○ suffix
- ○ root word

5 What would be a good title for the following category of actions?
tearing–breaking–cutting–ripping–crumpling
- ○ Combination Reactions
- ○ Replacement Reactions
- ○ Physical Changes
- ○ Chemical Reactions

6 Which word would finish this analogy?
Physical change is to **cutting** as **chemical change** is to _____.
- ○ throwing away
- ○ burning
- ○ tearing
- ○ covering

7 You have to be **cautious** when making chemical reactions.
Which word is a synonym for the word "cautious"?
- ○ careless
- ○ careful
- ○ hazardous
- ○ smart

Integrating Science with Reading Instruction · 5–6 © 2002 Creative Teaching Press

Name _____ Date _____

Get Logical

The Learning Lab is a popular place for budding scientists to conduct experiments on matter. Yesterday in the lab, Josh, Megan, Alice, Jessica, and Dan were safely experimenting. Each young scientist was investigating one of the following changes to matter: physical change, combination reaction, decomposition reaction, single replacement reaction, and double replacement reaction. Use the clues below to decide which change to matter each young scientist was investigating.

Clues

❶ One young scientist wadded up her piece of gum and threw it in the trashcan.

❷ A male student experimented with putting carbon with oxygen to make carbon dioxide (CO_2).

❸ Dan's experiment involved acids and bases balancing each other out and switching places.

❹ It was not Megan who experimented with a combination reaction. She did just the opposite in the Learning Lab.

❺ Alice was not the female who investigated the physical change to matter.

	Josh	Megan	Alice	Jessica	Dan
Physical Change					
Combination Reaction					
Decomposition Reaction					
Single Replacement					
Double Replacement					

Josh was investigating _____.

Megan was investigating _____.

Alice was investigating _____.

Jessica was investigating _____.

Dan was investigating _____.

Physical and Chemical Changes

How are physical changes different from chemical changes?

Teacher Background Information

The main thing to keep in mind is that a physical change does not create any new substances. Mixtures and solutions are examples of physical changes. No energy, such as heat or electricity, is given off or required when a mixture is formed. In a mixture, the amounts of any one substance are not definite and can vary from time to time. You cannot write a chemical formula for a mixture. It would be like making a cake without measuring any of the ingredients. You can always separate the ingredients in a mixture. This can usually be done by sifting, by filtering, or by evaporation. A few types of mixtures are harder to separate. You cannot separate the ingredients of a solution by filtering.

Chemical changes always create new and different substances. Energy is always released or required for the chemical reaction to take place. Chemical changes always occur with fixed amounts of each ingredient. For example, water is always H_2O, meaning that two atoms of hydrogen will always combine with one atom of oxygen to create a molecule of water. A chemical change is equivalent to making a cake where you measure each ingredient. Chemical reactions tell us what type of chemical change has occurred. In combination reactions, new substances are formed from simpler parts. One common type of combination reaction is combustion. This occurs when something burns, as it is combining with oxygen. Decomposition reactions are the reverse. They result in simpler products than what you started with. Replacement reactions are just exchanges of components from one substance to another. Be sure students wash their hands after the experiment with copper sulfate. Copper sulfate can be purchased at a hardware or chemical supply store.

Experiment Results

Students should be able to separate all of the components of the mixture in Experiment A. They can pick out the marbles with their fingers. If they filter the remaining mixture, they will separate the water from the sand/iron filings mix. The iron filings can be separated from the sand with the use of the magnet. None of the materials will change during this experiment. This experiment demonstrates a physical change because students will still have the same ingredients they started with, and the properties will not change. After they sand the nail in Experiment B, it should look shiny. After 5 minutes in the copper sulfate solution, the nail will be covered with copper. Students can easily remove this copper with their fingers. The materials will change in this experiment. The nail will look very different from before. This is an example of a chemical change. Something new and different will be created. This is an example of a replacement reaction. Elemental copper will come out of the solution and coat the nail. Some of the iron from the nail will replace the copper in the solution.

Integrating Science with Reading Instruction · 5–6 © 2002 Creative Teaching Press

Physical and Chemical Changes

How are physical changes different from chemical changes?

Procedure

Experiment A (water, sand, marbles, iron filings)

1 Make a mixture of water, sand, marbles, and some iron filings in a cup. Stir the mixture with a spoon. Then, remove the spoon. Observe how the mixture looks.

2 Use the other cup, tweezers, the spoon, filter paper, the funnel, and/or the magnet to separate each ingredient, and set the ingredients on a paper towel.

3 Fold the filter paper in half and then in half again. Open it up into a cone shape, and place it in the funnel. Now, try to separate the mixture using the filter paper and funnel.

4 Observe each substance again after you complete steps 2 and 3.

Experiment B (nail and copper sulfate)

1 Rub the nail firmly with the steel wool to clean off the surface.

2 Fill a glass with one cup of <u>warm</u> water. Add 2 teaspoons (10 mL) of copper sulfate crystals to the glass. Stir to dissolve them.

3 Place the nail into the copper sulfate solution. Wait 5 minutes.

4 Use the tweezers to gently remove the nail from the solution. Lay the nail on a paper towel. Observe how it looks and feels.

5 Wash off the nail, the tweezers, and your hands.

MATERIALS

(per group)
- ✔ water
- ✔ sand
- ✔ 2 marbles
- ✔ iron filings
- ✔ 2 cups
- ✔ spoon
- ✔ tweezers
- ✔ filter paper
- ✔ funnel
- ✔ magnet
- ✔ nail
- ✔ steel wool
- ✔ glass
- ✔ copper sulfate
- ✔ teaspoon
- ✔ paper towels

Integrating Science with Reading Instruction · 5–6 © 2002 Creative Teaching Press

Name _____   Date _____

Physical and Chemical Changes

How are physical changes different from chemical changes?

Results and Conclusions

Experiment A (water, sand, marbles, iron filings)

1 Did you separate all of the substances to prove that the assortment of marbles, sand, water, and iron filings was a mixture? _____

2 Did the materials change during part of the experiment? _____
If so, how?

_____

3 Was this an example of a physical change or a chemical change? _____
Why do you think so?

_____

Experiment B (nail and copper sulfate)

1 How did the nail look after it was sanded to remove the dirt and oil?

_____

2 How did the nail look and feel after 5 minutes in the copper sulfate solution?

_____

3 Was this an example of a physical change or a chemical change? _____
Why do you think so?

_____

4 How are physical changes different from chemical changes?

_____

Integrating Science with Reading Instruction · 5–6 © 2002 Creative Teaching Press

Catch a Clue

What will we learn about in our reading today?

elements
and compounds

medicines

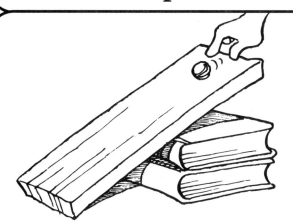

simple machines

electricity

Our Clues

1 It is related to the area of physical science.

2 We will learn about how things we use in our lives are created.

3 It involves some things that we use every day but are made out of things we usually do not see.

4 This area of science is vital in the world of chemistry.

Concept Map

Facts we already know about **elements and compounds,** and the new facts we have learned

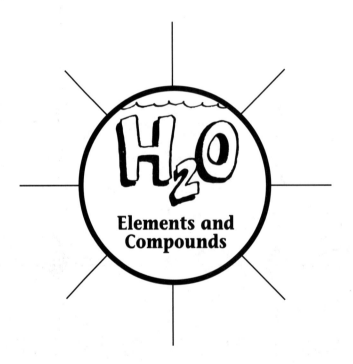

H₂O

Elements and Compounds

Integrating Science with Reading Instruction · 5–6 © 2002 Creative Teaching Press

Word Warm-Up

A B C D E F G H I J
CO_2 dad NaCl feed H_2O head

Which words might you expect to find in a story about **elements and compounds?**

chemical	homework	molecule
material	symbols	Latin
compounds	ingredients	characteristics
formula	elements	rainbow

Elements and Compounds

Do you remember when you first learned to read? First, you learned the letters of the alphabet. Then, you learned how to put letters together to form words. Learning about elements and compounds works in this same way.

Elements and compounds are a part of a subject called chemistry. Chemistry is the study of matter. All substances are made out of matter. Matter can be a solid, a liquid, or a gas. All matter is made up of smaller pieces called molecules. Molecules are made up of even smaller pieces called atoms. The "letters" of the chemistry alphabet are called elements. Each element is made up of only one kind of material. Scientists have identified and named over 100 elements. These are the "letters" that are used to make chemistry "words."

Chemists use abbreviations, or symbols, to stand for the names of chemical elements. It saves them a lot of time when writing the names of elements. Scientists have different ways of giving a chemical element a symbol. They usually take the first letter of an element's name and write it as a capital letter (e.g., H for hydrogen). If a letter has already been used to name another chemical element, they may create a symbol using the Latin name of the chemical (e.g., Au for gold which comes from its Latin name Aurum). Sometimes, they will use two letters for the symbol—a capital letter followed by a lowercase letter (e.g., Ca for calcium).

Now you are ready to make some chemistry words! Just like you combine letters to make words, you combine elements to make compounds, or chemistry words. Compounds are made when many elements combine to make new substances. It is like baking a cake. If you combine flour, eggs, sugar, chocolate, butter, and water and then place the mixture in an oven to bake, you can make a cake. The cake is very different from the separate ingredients you began with. After the cake is baked, you cannot reach into the cake and remove the eggs. In the same way, when elements

Integrating Science with Reading Instruction · 5–6 © 2002 Creative Teaching Press

combine to make a compound, you cannot easily separate the ingredients either. You have made something new. You have made a compound.

A compound is made of molecules. A molecule is made of more than one atom. You can have molecules made of just one type of atom, like an oxygen molecule, O_2. However, most molecules are made of many different kinds of atoms, just like most words are made of many different letters. Each time a chemist writes a capital letter, it stands for one atom of that element. If more than one atom is needed, then the chemist will write a little number next to the letter. For example, water would be written as H_2O. The H stands for hydrogen, the 2 means two atoms of hydrogen are needed, and the O stands for one atom of oxygen.

When you write a chemistry word, chemists call that a formula for a compound. Every chemical compound has a unique set of molecules that have different physical and chemical characteristics. When a compound is made, the original elements do <u>not</u> stay the same. For example, table salt is a compound. It is made up of two poisonous elements (sodium and chlorine). But, they are not poisonous when combined. In fact, table salt (NaCl) is essential to life. Some other common compounds are baking soda ($NaHCO_3$), brown sugar ($C_6H_{12}O_6$), and carbon dioxide (CO_2).

On the other hand, the ingredients in "mixtures" <u>do</u> keep their same characteristics. Mixtures are just an assortment of elements or elements and compounds that have been placed or mixed together but were not combined. Soil, ocean water, and air are examples of mixtures. It is easier to separate the elements of mixtures than compounds. Chemists use different combinations of elements, mixtures, and compounds to create medicines, spices, soaps, flavorings, and other products that we use every day.

$NaHCO_3$

$C_6H_{12}O_6$

$NaCl$

Integrating Science with Reading Instruction · 5–6 © 2002 Creative Teaching Press

Comprehension Questions

? Literal Questions

1. What is an element?
2. What are the three states of matter?
3. What makes up chemistry "words"? Give two specific examples.
4. What is the difference between a mixture and a compound?
5. How is a pure element different from an element in a compound?

? Inferential Questions

1. How is the organization of matter the same as learning how to read? Explain your reasoning.
2. When you write words, you use certain vowels more often than any consonants. In chemistry, certain elements are used more often, too. Did the story give you an idea of some commonly used elements? Name three examples.
3. What is the formula for one molecule of baking soda? Brown sugar?
4. What makes one compound different from another? Give some specific examples.
5. Why is chemistry important?

? Making Connections

1. What types of things have you mixed together? Did you make a mixture or a compound? How do you know?
2. What do chemists do? Why are their jobs important? How do they affect your life?
3. Is it easier to read letters or words? Do you think that it is easier to read elements or formulas? What role do the letters and numbers play in a scientific formula?
4. *Super Sid the Science Kid* is a new television show on cable TV. Every day he conducts physical science experiments. What materials do you think the Science Kid uses?
5. If you had the opportunity to conduct any chemistry experiment, what would you want to do? Would it be safe or dangerous? What precautions would you take?

Integrating Science with Reading Instruction · 5–6 © 2002 Creative Teaching Press

Sharpen Your Skills

1 Below you will see part of a telephone directory under the listing of "chemists."
What street does Dr. Gold work on?

Barium, Dr.	Shiny Street	555-5493
Carbon, Dr.	Black Avenue	555-3945
Feldspar, Dr.	Calico Corner	555-7777
Gold, Dr.	Toothy Trail	555-9435
Limestone, Dr.	Green Lane	555-6565

    ○ Shiny Street   ○ Calico Corner
    ○ Green Lane   ○ Toothy Trail

2 If you gave Dr. Carbon a nickname that uses the scientific element symbol for his last name, what would you call him?

    ○ Dr. Car   ○ Dr. Bon
    ○ Dr. Ca   ○ Dr. C

3 Every chemical compound has a unique set of molecules that have different physical and chemical **properties.**

Which word is a synonym for the word "properties"?

    ○ homes   ○ characteristics
    ○ problems   ○ reactions

4 When elements combine to make a compound, you cannot **easily** separate the ingredients.

In this sentence, what part of speech is the word "easily"?

    ○ adjective   ○ adverb
    ○ preposition   ○ conjunction

5 Which of the following is an anagram for the word "salt"?

    ○ NaCl   ○ last
    ○ pepper   ○ sweet and lasting treat

6 Which words would finish this analogy?

Elements are to _____ as **letters** are to _____.

    ○ elements/words   ○ compounds/words
    ○ words/light-years   ○ grains of sand/elements

Name _____   Date _____

In chemistry class, five students are each studying a different formula to conduct an experiment. The five students are Lacey, Sean, Emma, MacKenzie, and Jake. Use the clues below to determine which formula each student used to conduct his or her experiment.

Clues

❶ Sean's formula did not have any atoms of oxygen.

❷ The formula MacKenzie investigated did not have any atoms of the element carbon.

❸ A female student investigated a formula with the element hydrogen.

❹ There were six atoms of two different elements in the formula investigated by a female, but it was not Lacey.

❺ Jake's formula did not have any chlorine or hydrogen involved.

	Lacey	Sean	Emma	MacKenzie	Jake
H_2O					
$C_6H_{12}O_6$					
CO_2					
$NaHCO_3$					
$NaCl$					

Lacey investigated _____.

Sean investigated _____.

Emma investigated _____.

MacKenzie investigated _____.

Jake investigated _____.

Integrating Science with Reading Instruction · 5–6 © 2002 Creative Teaching Press

Elements and Compounds

How are elements different from compounds?

Teacher Background Information

It is helpful if students understand the way chemists use symbols to represent elements in writing chemical formulas for compounds. Students are naturally curious about which chemicals common items are made of. The hardest aspect for most students to understand is what makes one element different from another.

Each element is made of a particular type of atom. What makes one kind of atom different from another is the number of protons in the nucleus of the atom. Atoms themselves are composed of three types of particles—protons, neutrons, and electrons. Protons and neutrons are found in the center, or nucleus, of the atom. The number of protons (positively charged particles) an atom has is called its "atomic number." Every element has a different number of protons, starting with hydrogen that has an atomic number of 1. Neutral atoms have the same number of electrons as protons. Electrons are extremely small negatively charged particles that orbit around the nucleus of the atom. Most atoms also have neutral particles in their nucleus called neutrons. It is the electrons that determine if a chemical element will react with something else to form a compound. There are several shells or orbital rings that the electrons travel in. If the outermost shell is completely full of electrons, then the element is not reactive. Most elements have outer electron shells that are not full. The element is looking to share, pick up, or lose electrons to become more stable. This is what makes most elements enter into chemical reactions. Everyday objects can be used as samples of elements and compounds. A penny is made of copper. Copper wire can be obtained from a hardware store. Paper clips are made of iron. Fishing weights are made of lead. Charcoal is made of carbon. The yellow end of fireplace matches is made of sulfur. Aluminum foil is a convenient source of aluminum.

Experiment Results

Students should indicate on their Elements and Compounds Chart (page 143) that copper, carbon, aluminum, iron, sulfur, and lead are elements. All of the other samples are compounds. Of the sample elements, all are metals except for sulfur. The magnet will pick up the paper clip because it is made of iron and magnets are attracted to elemental iron. However, the magnet will not be attracted to the iron tablet because this iron is part of a compound. It now has new and different properties. The students should learn that elements are made up of only one substance, whereas compounds are made of several elements that have been combined.

Integrating Science with Reading Instruction · 5–6 © 2002 Creative Teaching Press

Elements and Compounds

How are elements different from compounds?

Procedure

❶ Place all of the solid chemical samples and the cup of water on the tray. Set the bar magnet off to the side. Observe all of the samples.

❷ Use your Elements and Compounds Chart to sort the samples into two groups—elements and compounds.

❸ Now observe the elements more closely. Sort them into metals and nonmetals. Look for some characteristics of metals (e.g., shiny, can change their shape).

❹ Now observe the compounds more closely. Your chart lists the elements in each compound.

❺ Use the bar magnet to try to pick up the paper clip.

❻ Use the bar magnet to try to pick up the iron supplement tablet.

MATERIALS

(per group)
- ✔ Elements and Compounds Chart (page 143)
- ✔ solid chemical samples
  - copper
  - sugar cube
  - carbon
  - aluminum
  - iron
  - lead
  - baking soda
  - chalk
  - sulfur
  - table salt
- ✔ cup of water
- ✔ tray
- ✔ bar magnet
- ✔ paper clip
- ✔ iron supplement tablet (ferrous sulfate)

Integrating Science with Reading Instruction · 5–6 © 2002 Creative Teaching Press

Name _____   Date _____

Elements and Compounds Chart

How are elements different from compounds?

Directions: Place check marks in the appropriate boxes to indicate how you sorted your samples.

Sample	Symbol or Formula	Element	Compound	Metal	Nonmetal
Copper	Cu				
Sugar Cube	$C_{12}H_{22}O_{11}$				
Carbon	C				
Aluminum	Al				
Baking Soda	$NaHCO_3$				
Water	H_2O				
Iron	Fe				
Table Salt	NaCl				
Sulfur	S				
Chalk	$CaCO_3$				
Iron Tablet	$FeSO_4$				
Lead	Pb				

Name _____   Date _____

Elements and Compounds

How are elements different from compounds?

Results and Conclusions

❶ Which samples were elements?

_____

❷ Which samples were compounds?

_____

❸ Which samples were metals?

_____

❹ Which samples were nonmetals?

_____

❺ Did the magnet pick up the paper clip? _____

Why or why not?

_____

❻ Did the magnet pick up the iron tablet? _____

Why or why not?

_____

❼ How are elements different from compounds?

_____

Integrating Science with Reading Instruction · 5–6 © 2002 Creative Teaching Press

Answer Key

Page 9

ecosystems

Page 11

All words should be chosen.

Page 14

Literal Questions
1. groups of life forms that interact with each other and the nonliving parts of the environment
2. climate and soil type
3. hardwood, evergreen, and tropical rain forest
4. help clean the air, provide homes for wildlife, and supply people with fruits, nuts, and medicine
5. forest, coastal, desert, grassland, tundra, freshwater, and ocean

Inferential Questions
Answers will vary. Accept all reasonable responses.

Making Connections
Answers will vary. Accept all reasonable responses.

Page 15

1. following
2. encyclopedia
3. adjective
4. salt/honey
5. homonyms
6. environment
7. quotation marks

Page 16

Joe's group—Desert
Michelle's group—Tropical Rain Forest
Steven's group—Tundra
Sheri's group—Coastal Ecosystems
Lenny's group—Ocean

Page 20

Answers will vary. Possible answers include:
1. The amount of water caused very little grass to sprout.
2. The amount of water did not affect the growth of the cacti.
3. The amount of water allowed the majority of the grass seed to sprout.
4. The amount of water caused the cacti to become soft and begin to rot.
5. Yes, because cacti grow better in sandy soil were the water is not easily absorbed.
6. Yes, because grass requires soil that easily absorbs water.
7. grassland
8. desert
9. Plants will only be found within a climate or soil type that fits its specific needs.

Page 21

animal classification

Page 23

All words should be chosen.

Page 26

Literal Questions
1. vertebrates, invertebrates; invertebrates
2. **vertebrates**—backbone, internal skeletal structure, smallest group
   invertebrates—lacks a backbone, largest group
   similarities—some vertebrates are cold-blooded, living animals, five main classification groups
3. sponges, worms, echinoderms, mollusks, and arthropods
4. fish, amphibians, reptiles, birds, and mammals
5. about 9 million

Inferential Questions
Answers will vary. Accept all reasonable responses.

Making Connections
Answers will vary. Accept all reasonable responses.

Page 27

1. 2
2. fish
3. hundred
4. clas-si-fi-ca-tion
5. vertebrates/animal
6. invertebrates
7. living things

Page 28

Millipedes–Blue Wall
Rabbits–Red Wall
Salamanders–Yellow Wall
Sponges–Green Wall
Ostrich–Orange Wall

Page 31

Answers will vary. Possible answers include:
sea sponge–invertebrate, no legs, soft, springy, or slightly rough
earthworm–invertebrate, no legs, soft, smooth, and moist with tiny hairs
spider–invertebrate, 8 legs, dry
insect–invertebrate, 6 legs, dry
fish–vertebrate, no legs, wet, soft, slimy

Page 32

Answers will vary. Possible answers include:
1. allow water to pass through
2. 2; 3; number of legs
3. wet scales; provides protection
4. The fish is a vertebrate.
5. to breathe
6. shape, number of appendages, body covering, and skeleton

Page 33

photosynthesis

Page 35

All words should be chosen.

Page 38

Literal Questions
1. to make something with light
2. chlorophyll, carbon dioxide, water, and solar energy
3. release of large amounts of water vapor
4. phloem tubes; carry food that is made in the leaves down to other parts of the plant
5. release oxygen the plant does not need as well as excess water

Inferential Questions
Answers will vary. Accept all reasonable responses.

Making Connections
Answers will vary. Accept all reasonable responses.

Page 39

1. across
2. homophones
3. pho-to-syn-the-sis
4. release
5. xylem
6. Requirements
7. healthiest

Page 4

Rachel–Water
Brian–Energy
Sheila–Chlorophyll
Tom–Carbon Dioxide
Raymond–Xylem

Page 43

Answers will vary. Possible answers include:
1. **celery**–green to orange-green; will vary based on sample size
   carrot–orange-green; will vary
   green onion–orange-green; will vary
   apple–reddish-orange; should have the most simple sugar
   rice–may change to a slightly different shade of blue; no simple sugar
   table sugar–blue; no simple sugar
2. celery; carrot
3. green part of the green onion
4. apple; rice grains
5. yes; rice grain; almost all the sugar has been converted into starch
6. by testing for the presence of simple sugar

Page 44

body systems

Page 46

All words should be chosen except *telephone* and *magazine*.

Page 49

Literal Questions
1. organ system
2. **skeletal**–allows you to move, protects vital organs
   respiratory–inhale oxygen, exhale carbon dioxide
   nervous–most complex and fragile, sends messages from the brain to other parts of the body
   muscle–covers the skeleton,

two different types of muscles
digestive—breaks down food, absorbs nutrients from food
circulatory—heart pumps blood to the body through arteries, veins return blood to the heart
excretory—removes and eliminates waste from the body
endocrine—produce hormones to regulate growth and development
reproductive—allows people to have babies, different in males and females
3. nervous system
4. **voluntary**—lip and arm muscles; **involuntary**—heart, involuntary muscles that cause goose bumps
5. The spinal cord recognizes a familiar message and sends a response to the body without first sending the message to the brain—this is called a reflex. The body responds so quickly because it doesn't think about it.

Inferential Questions
Answers will vary. Accept all reasonable responses.
Making Connections
Answers will vary. Accept all reasonable responses.

1. The heart/pumps blood throughout your body.
2. necessary
3. They think he will be healthy once again.
4. dictionary
5. irony
6. muscular system
7. tissues

Dr. Able—Heart Surgery
Dr. Help—Respiratory Care
Dr. Better—Digestive Disorders
Dr. Care—Bones and Joints
Dr. Love—Brain Surgery

Answers will vary. Possible answers include:
1. chest cavity with the rib cage
2. windpipe or trachea
3. bronchial tubes
4. the lungs; No, the lungs are made of tiny air sacs called alveoli, which look like clusters of grapes.
5. the diaphragm
6. The small balloons inflate.; Air pressure is greater outside the balloons which forces air into the balloons.
7. The small balloons deflate.; Increased air pressure within the balloons, as compared to the outside, forces the air out of the balloons.
8. The diaphragm helps to increase or decrease air pressure within the lungs to allow people to breathe.

our Moon

All words should be chosen except *cookies* and *bicycle*.

Literal Questions
1. In a lunar eclipse the Earth passes between the Sun and the Moon, the Earth blocks the Sun's light creating a shadow over the Moon.; In a solar eclipse, the Moon passes between the Earth and the Sun.
2. flat plains, mountains, and craters; light and dark patches of shadow from the plains, mountains, and craters
3. new moon, waxing crescent, first quarter, waxing gibbous, full moon, waning gibbous, last quarter, waning crescent; The different shapes of the Moon are related to the positions of the Moon, the Earth, and the Sun.
4. newspaper or the Internet; an almanac
5. waxing (appearing), waning (disappearing)
Inferential Questions
Answers will vary. Accept all reasonable responses.
Making Connections
Answers will vary. Accept all reasonable responses.

1. figurative
2. homonym
3. stands in the way of
4. waxing gibbous
5. waning
6. waxing gibbous
7. encyclopedia

Page 62

Sylvia—Gibbous Moon
Courtney—Waxing Moon
Emily—Waning Moon
Dylan—New Moon
Tobias—Full Moon

Page 65

Answers will vary. Possible answers include:

1. yes
2. Yes, because the "space alien" students are able to see the other sides of the Moon.
3. Yes, because only one side of the Moon is ever visible to the "Earth" student.
4. The Moon takes as long to rotate as it does to revolve around the Earth.
5. the Earth is between the Sun and the Moon
6. the Moon is between the Earth and the Sun
7. The Sun, the Moon, and the Earth are in a straight alignment and the light behind the Moon and the Earth is blocked.
8. The Moon rotates as it revolves around the Earth. During a new moon, the Moon is between the Earth and the Sun, so light does not reach the side of the Moon that's visible from Earth. When a full moon is visible, the Earth is between the Sun and the Moon, allowing the Sun to shine on the side of the Moon that is visible from Earth.

Page 66

outer space

Page 68

All words should be chosen.

Page 71

Literal Questions

1. No one knows how large our universe is. The frame of reference used in the story is one grain of sand—the distance between the Earth and the Sun is one grain of sand. Using the sand as a comparison, Pluto would be 30 feet away.
2. galaxies, planets, constellations, nebulae, comets, asteroids, and meteors
3. Asteroids are larger than meteors.
4. constellations; Big Dipper and Little Dipper; a meteor that enters the Earth's atmosphere at a high speed and burns up
5. Edmund Halley; Halley's Comet; Edmund Halley predicted that the comet would return

Inferential Questions

Answers will vary. Accept all reasonable responses.

Making Connections

Answers will vary. Accept all reasonable responses.

Page 72

1. material left over
2. Internet
3. tightly
4. conjunction
5. solar system
6. light-years
7. star

Page 73

Luke—Nebulae
Walker—Galaxies
Obie—Stars
Dewey—Comets
Hailey—Planets

Page 77

Answers will vary. Possible answers include:

1. most of outer space is dark and black
2. Asteroids are much bigger than meteors.
3. Nebulae are clouds in outer space, and the smudge of chalk gives a "cloudy" appearance.
4. irregular shapes of dust and gases
5. A comet's orbit is not equidistant from the Sun. One end of the orbit is close to the Sun while the other end is far away from the Sun.
6. galaxies, constellations, nebulae, comets, asteroids, and meteors

Page 78

weathering and erosion

Page 80

All words should be chosen except farmer.

Page 83

Literal Questions

1. Weathering is the breaking down or wearing away of the Earth's surface and erosion moves broken-down bits to another location.
2. physical and chemical; **Physical weathering** occurs when rocks and minerals crumble into smaller pieces. **Chemical weathering** occurs when rocks break down due to a chemical reaction and minerals in the rock change.; **physical**—when larger rocks are broken into smaller and smaller rocks, **chemical**—nail that becomes rusty
3. anywhere; appearance of the landscape changes over time
4. plant trees or other vegetation along a hillside slope or add bark chips or crushed tree leaves to the soil in a garden
5. When water in a cave drips and evaporates, it leaves behind hardened limestone hanging down from either the ceiling or sticking up from the cave floor.

Inferential Questions

Answers will vary. Accept all reasonable responses.

Making Connections

Answers will vary. Accept all reasonable responses.

Page 84

1. break down
2. weath-er-ing
3. weathering
4. adverb
5. She needed to pound the bricks into the dirt to make her planter.
6. blow away
7. clay

Page 85

Javier—Chemical Weathering
Anthony—Erosion
Dawn—Earth's Elements
Emily—Physical Weathering
Emmet—Preventing Erosion

Page 88

Answers will vary. Possible answers include:

1. **shale**—smooth, **sandstone**—gritty, **limestone**—hard and rough
2. Yes; some of the rocks will have broken pieces
3. The "river rocks" have a rounded shape and a smoother surface texture.
4. physical weathering
5. caused tiny bubbles or fizzing to come from the chalk; happens in nature where limestone caves are formed; chemical weathering
6. The water washes away a portion of the "hilltop."; erosion
7. creates canyons, caves, or alters the shape of mountains and hillsides

Page 89

energy from the Earth

Page 91

All words should be chosen.

Page 94

Literal Questions

1. renewable and nonrenewable; Renewable resources are things that can replace themselves. Nonrenewable resources cannot be replaced or reproduced.
2. hydropower, wind energy, solar energy, tidal energy, and geothermal energy
3. wood
4. limiting the usage of nonrenewable resources; it allows nonrenewable resources to last longer
5. coal

Inferential Questions

Answers will vary. Accept all reasonable responses.

Making Connections

Answers will vary. Accept all reasonable responses.

Page 95

1. almanac
2. conjunction
3. natural gas
4. rain/coal
5. worries
6. reuse
7. eight

Page 96

Claymore—Oil
Riverdale—Wind Energy
Scottsberg—Natural Gas
Shrewsberry—Solar Energy
Thomasville—Wave Energy

Page 99

Answers will vary. Possible answers include:
1. The oil and water would not mix.
2. There's a thin layer of oil on top of the water.; Oil is less dense than water.
3. Yes; sandstone, shale, and limestone
4. sandstone
5. household oil
6. shale rock
7. shale rock
8. natural gas; Natural gas is lighter and will rise up as far as possible.
9. surface deposits have been used up

Page 100

pulley

Page 102

All words should be chosen except skateboard and library.

Page 105

Literal Questions
1. a simple machine; moves objects; allows people to easily lift or move heavy objects, used in exercise equipment
2. fixed pulley and moveable pulley; The pulleys are similar because they make work easier for a person to complete. The pulleys are different because the fixed pulley is attached and does not move, and the moveable pulley is attached to the object that is moving. Also, fixed pulleys change the direction of the work, but moveable pulleys do not change the direction of the work.
3. fixed pulley
4. Farmers use pulleys to raise hay bales, construction workers use them to move loads of materials, and rock climbers use pulleys to safely climb rocks.
5. Fixed pulleys make it easier to raise a flag on a flagpole—without the fixed pulley, a person would have to climb up and down the pole to attach the flag. Moveable pulleys make it easier to lift heavy objects like a bucket of bricks—without the moveable pulley a person would have to use their muscles to pull up the full weight of the bricks.

Inferential Questions
Answers will vary. Accept all reasonable responses.

Making Connections
Answers will vary. Accept all reasonable responses.

Page 106

1. use
2. construction worker
3. preposition
4. moving them with your hands
5. flag/bucket
6. capable of
7. pulley = less work

Page 107

Bobby—Combined Pulley
Darren—Wheel
Flo—Wedge
Heather—Fixed Pulley
Jared—Moveable Pulley

Page 110

Answers will vary. Possible answers include:
1. fixed pulley; It is not any easier to lift the bucket with or without the pulley.; The fixed pulley only changed the direction of the way the work was done (pulling down instead of up).
2. moveable; yes; The pulley is doing part of the work.
3. both; yes; Several moveable pulleys are being used which give an added mechanical advantage.
4. fixed pulleys—flag poles
single moveable pulleys—exercise equipment
block and tackle pulleys—construction cranes
5. Pulleys make it easier to lift, raise, or move objects from one place to another.

Page 111

heat energy

Page 113

All words should be chosen.

Page 116

Literal Questions
1. **conduction**—transfer of heat through solids
   convection—transfer of heat through liquids and gases
   radiation—transfer of heat through waves or particles
2. metal
3. wood or plastic
4. radiation; Radiation releases invisible heat rays that can travel, or radiate, through space where there are no air molecules.
5. the bottom

Inferential Questions
Answers will vary. Accept all reasonable responses.

Making Connections
Answers will vary. Accept all reasonable responses.

Page 117

1. conduction/convection
2. dictionary
3. transfer
4. conjunction
5. ruler
6. hot/cold
7. abbreviation

Page 118

Margo—Convection
Hector—Increasing Heat Energy
Tasha—Radiation
Kurran—Temperature
Sydney—Conduction

Page 121

Answers will vary. Possible answers include:
1. the vanes started to spin
2. to allow the heat to either be absorbed or reflected
3. the absorption of radiant energy on the black vanes
4. radiation
5. The wax bump melted.; Heat traveled through the nail causing it to warm up.
6. conduction
7. Answers will vary. Accept all reasonable responses.
8. The food coloring slowly mixed into the water.; The food coloring quickly mixed into the water.; Yes, the molecules in the hot water were moving faster than the molecules in the cold water, which caused the food coloring to mix faster in the hot water than in the cold water.
9. how the heat is transferred from the heat source

Page 122

physical and chemical changes

Page 124

All words should be chosen except lightning.

Page 127

Literal Questions
1. physical and chemical; physical—temporary, chemical—permanent
2. decomposition and combination reactions
3. when the original matter splits up into two or more compounds and/or elements; chemical
4. combination, decomposition, and replacement
5. crumble a piece of paper, stretch a rubber band, melt a piece of ice

Inferential Questions
Answers will vary. Accept all reasonable responses.

Making Connections
Answers will vary. Accept all reasonable responses.

Page 128

1. temporarily
2. pharmacist
3. com-bi-na-tion
4. suffix
5. Physical Changes
6. burning
7. careful

Page 129

Josh—Combination Reaction
Megan—Decomposition Reaction
Alice—Single Replacement
Jessica—Physical Change
Dan—Double Replacement

Page 132

Answers will vary. Possible answers include:

Experiment A
1. yes
2. no
3. physical change

Experiment B
1. shiny
2. The nail was covered with copper but the copper easily came off.
3. chemical change; The nail looked very different from before being placed into the copper sulfate.
4. In a physical change the material does not change. In a chemical change the material becomes something completely different.

Page 133

elements and compounds

Page 135

All words should be chosen except homework and rainbow.

Page 138

Literal Questions
1. An element is made up of only one kind of material.
2. solid, liquid, and gas
3. elements that are combined to make a compound; H_2O (2 hydrogen atoms + 1 oxygen atom) and NaCl (1 sodium atom + 1 chlorine atom)
4. Elements in a mixture keep their same characteristics and are easy to separate—elements in a compound form to create something new and cannot be easily separated.
5. An element in a compound has been changed in some way, and a pure element has not been changed.

Inferential Questions
Answers will vary. Accept all reasonable responses.

Making Connections
Answers will vary. Accept all reasonable responses.

Page 139

1. Toothy Trail
2. Dr. C
3. characteristics
4. adverb
5. last
6. compounds/words

Page 140

Lacey—$NaHCO_3$
Sean—NaCl
Emma—$C_6H_{12}O_6$
MacKenzie—H_2O
Jake—CO_2

Page 143

Copper, carbon, aluminum, iron, sulfur, and lead are elements. All the other samples are compounds. Of the sample elements, all are metals except sulfur.

Page 144

Answers will vary. Possible answers include:
1. copper, carbon, aluminum, iron, sulfur, lead
2. sugar cube, baking soda, water, table salt, chalk, iron tablet
3. copper, carbon, aluminum, iron, lead
4. sulfur
5. Yes; It is made of iron.
6. No; The iron is part of a compound.
7. Elements are made up of only one substance, whereas compounds are made of several elements that have been combined.